GRAFFITI GROOVE

Portraits of Hip-Hop Elegance Coloring Book

Bibliographical Note
Graffiti Groove Coloring Book is a new work,
first published by Amazon, Inc, in 2024

International Standard Book Number
ISBN: 9798877033986

Manufactured in US

Description:

"Dive into the vibrant world of urban beauty and street elegance with our coloring book, 'Graffiti Groove: Portraits of Hip-Hop Elegance.' This unique collection features a series of intricately designed illustrations, each portraying a beautiful hip-hop woman amidst the dynamic energy of the city streets. From bold graffiti backdrops to intricate street fashion details, this coloring book invites you to explore the fusion of style, rhythm, and self-expression.

Embark on a coloring journey where the concrete jungle meets the world of hip-hop, celebrating the essence of street culture. Immerse yourself in the intricate patterns of graffiti, the rhythm of urban beats, and the bold elegance of hip-hop fashion. Each page tells a story of individuality, strength, and creativity, waiting for your personal touch to bring it to life.

Whether you're a seasoned colorist or a newcomer to the world of adult coloring, 'Graffiti Groove' offers a canvas for self-expression and creativity. Unleash your imagination as you experiment with a spectrum of hues, creating a personalized masterpiece that captures the soul of hip-hop beauty. Get ready to infuse life into these dynamic portraits, where every stroke is a brushstroke on the canvas of urban art and style.

'Graffiti Groove: Portraits of Hip-Hop Elegance' is more than a coloring book; it's an invitation to explore, create, and celebrate the fusion of street culture and artistic expression. So, pick up your favorite coloring tools, embrace the rhythm, and let the streets come alive with your unique blend of color and creativity."

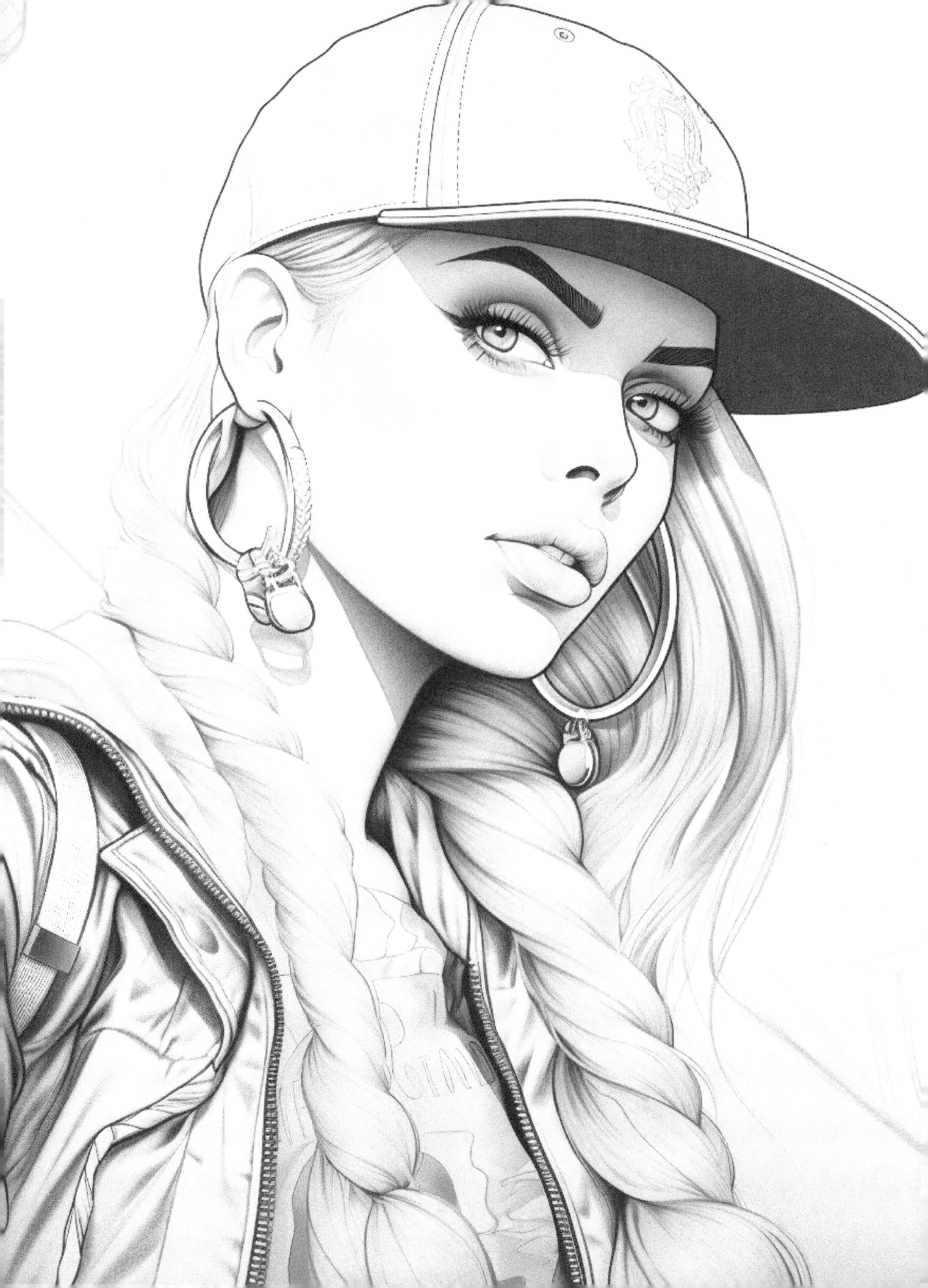

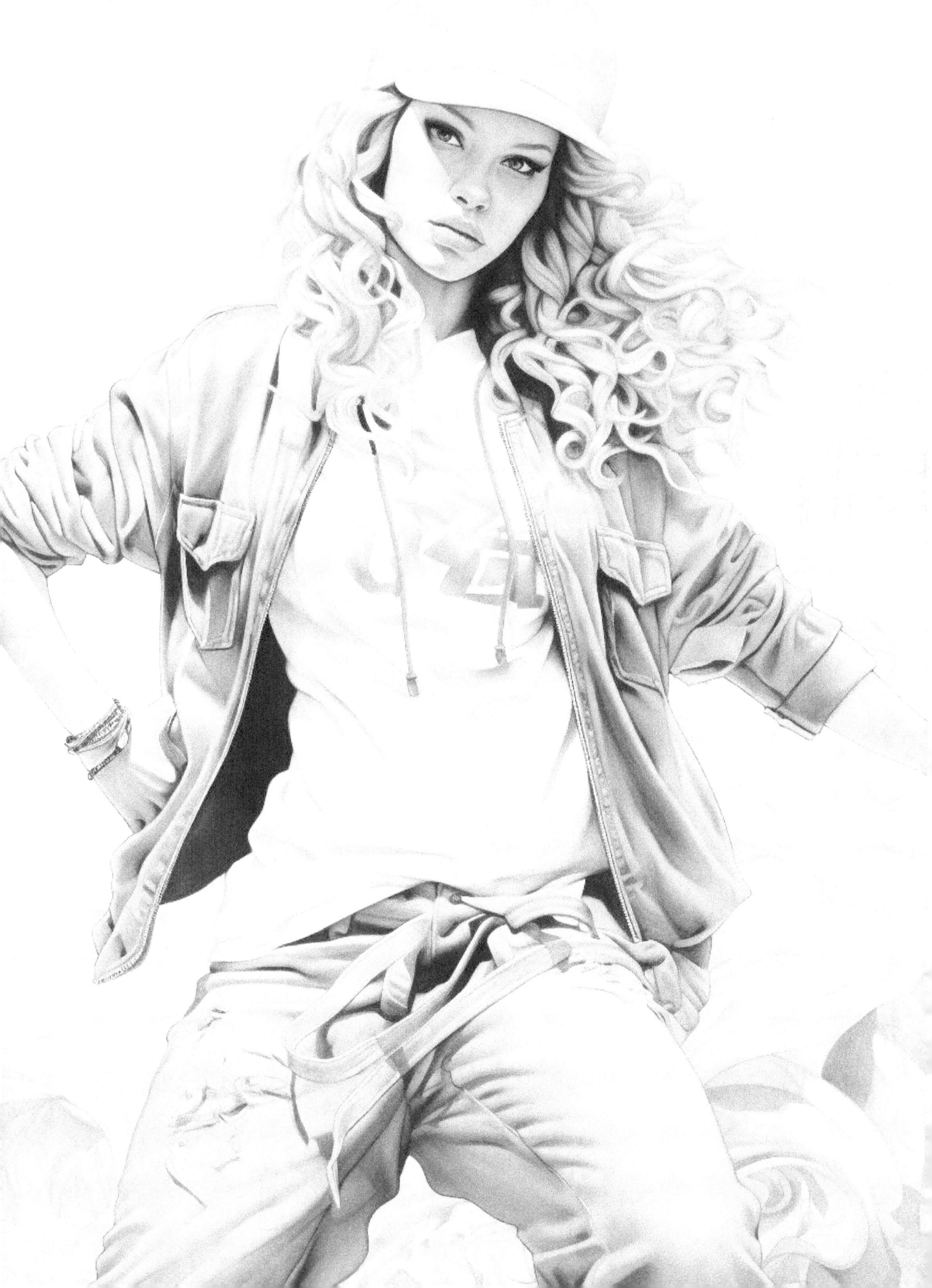

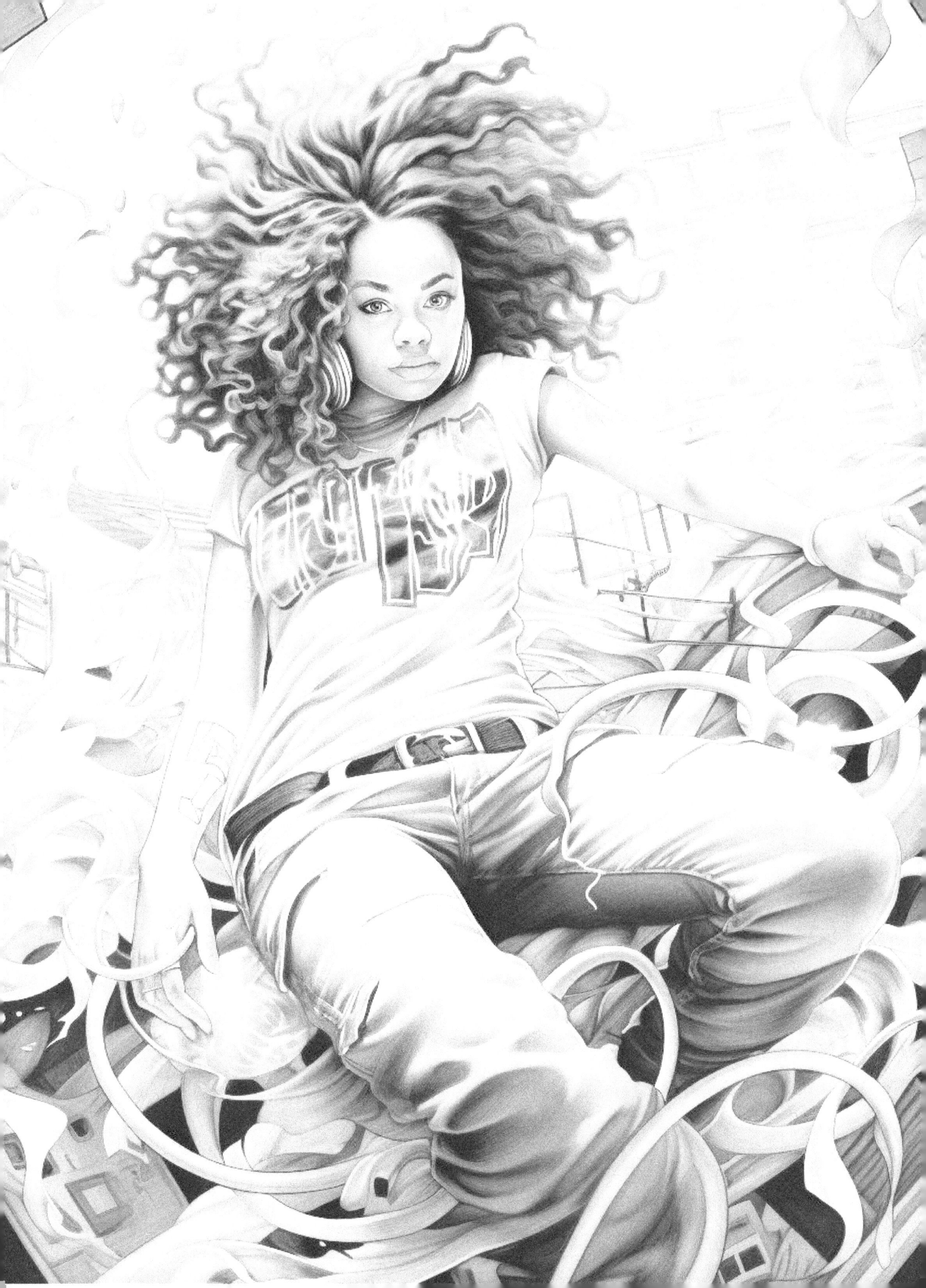

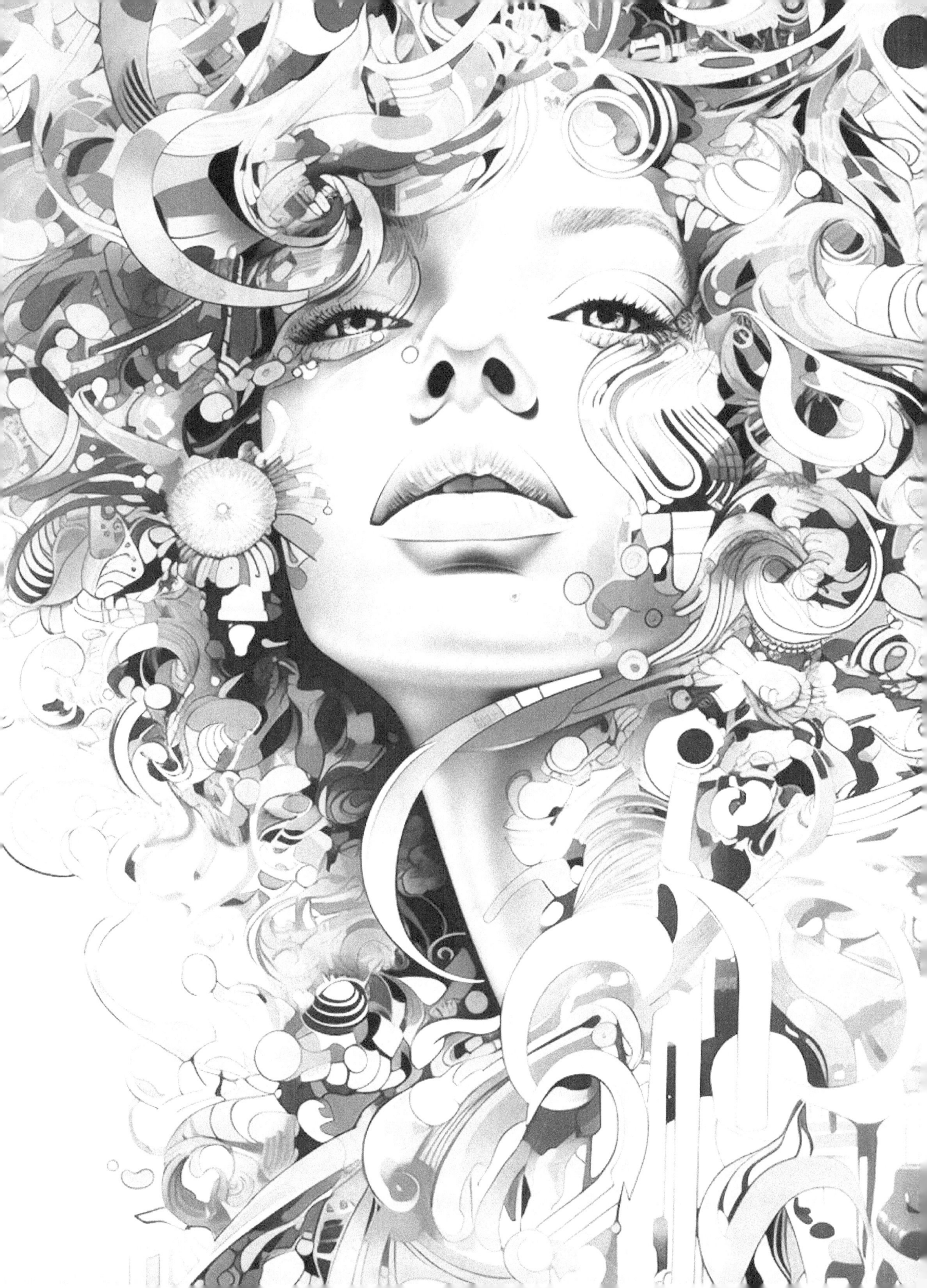

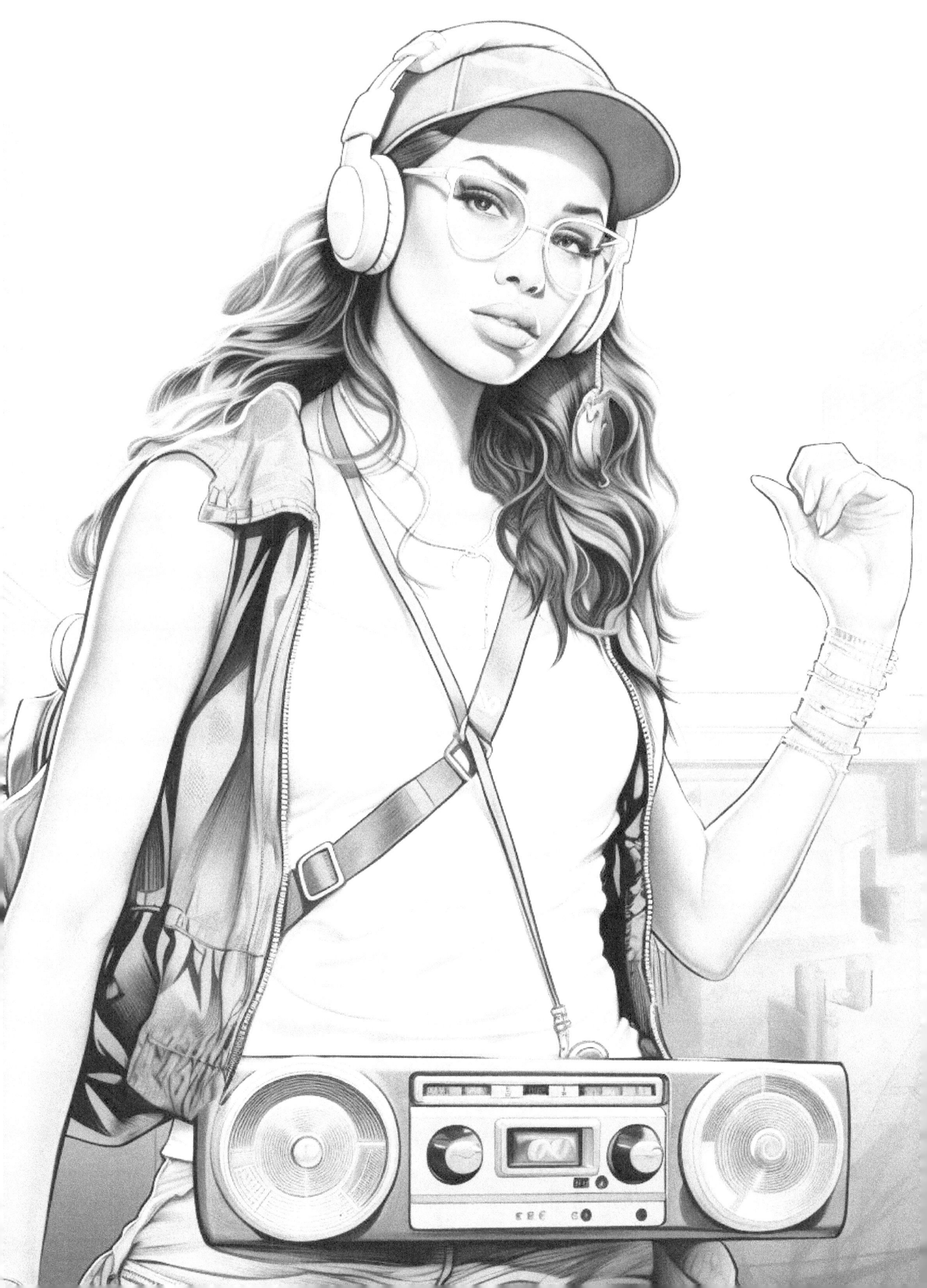

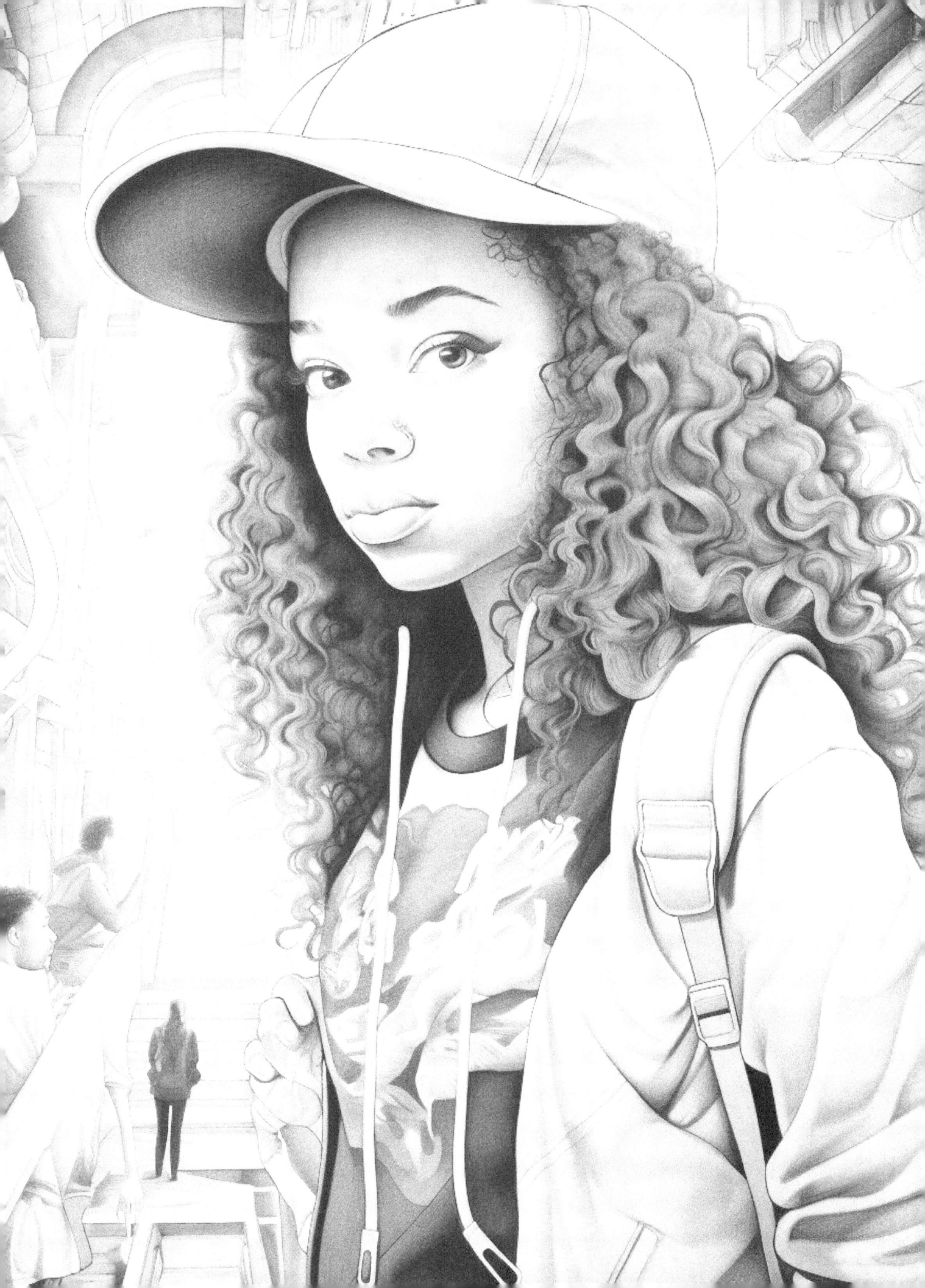

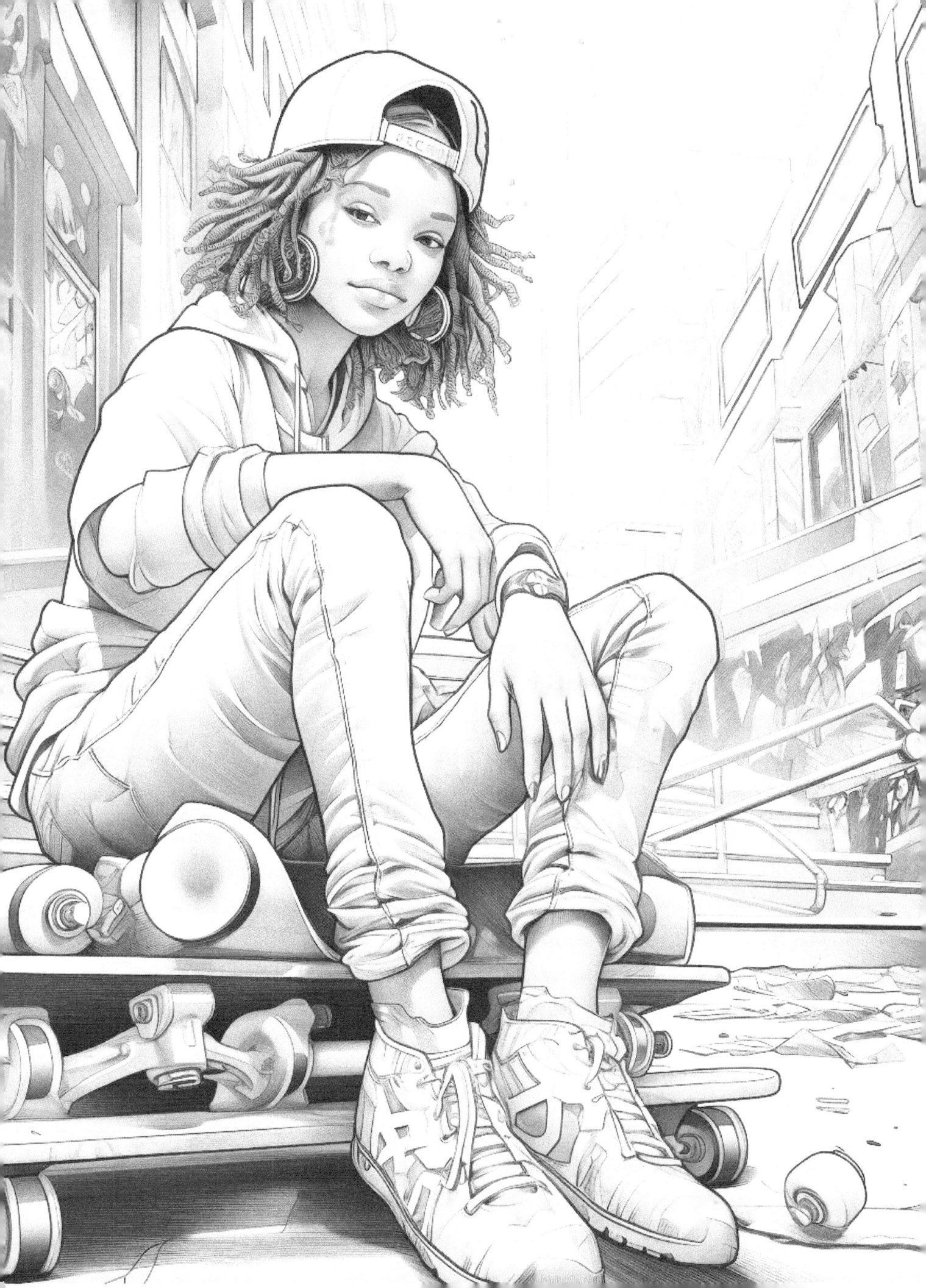

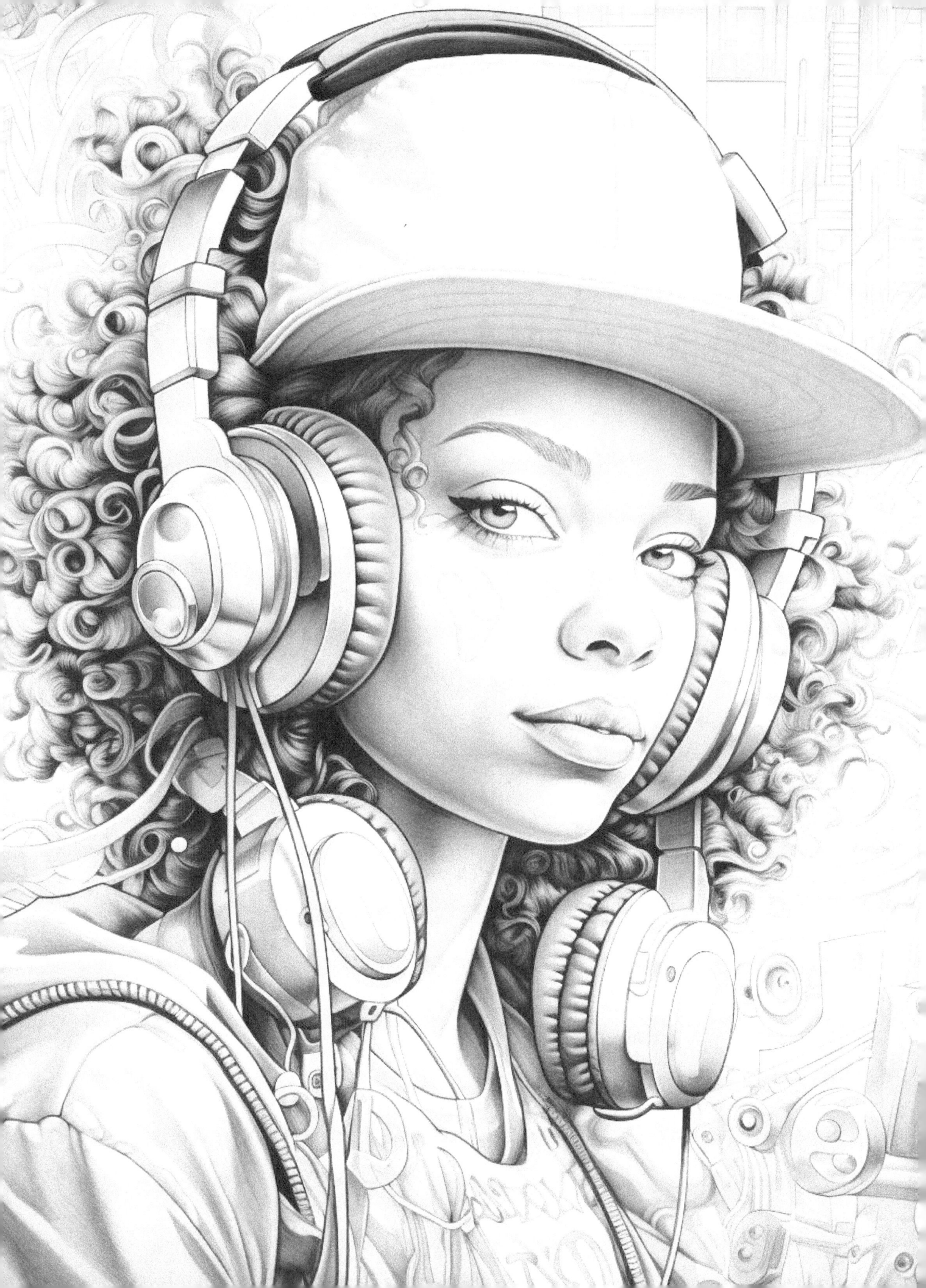

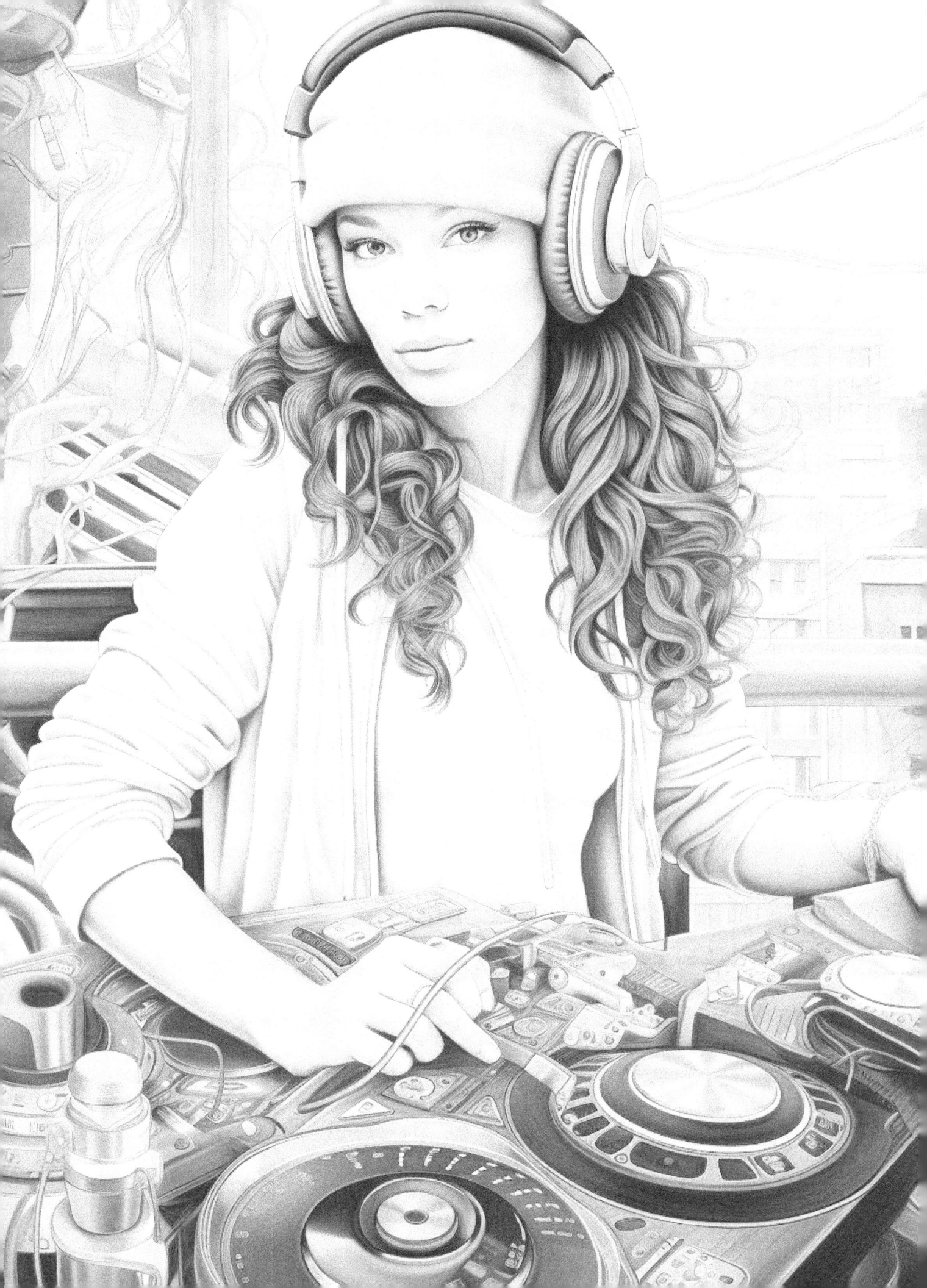

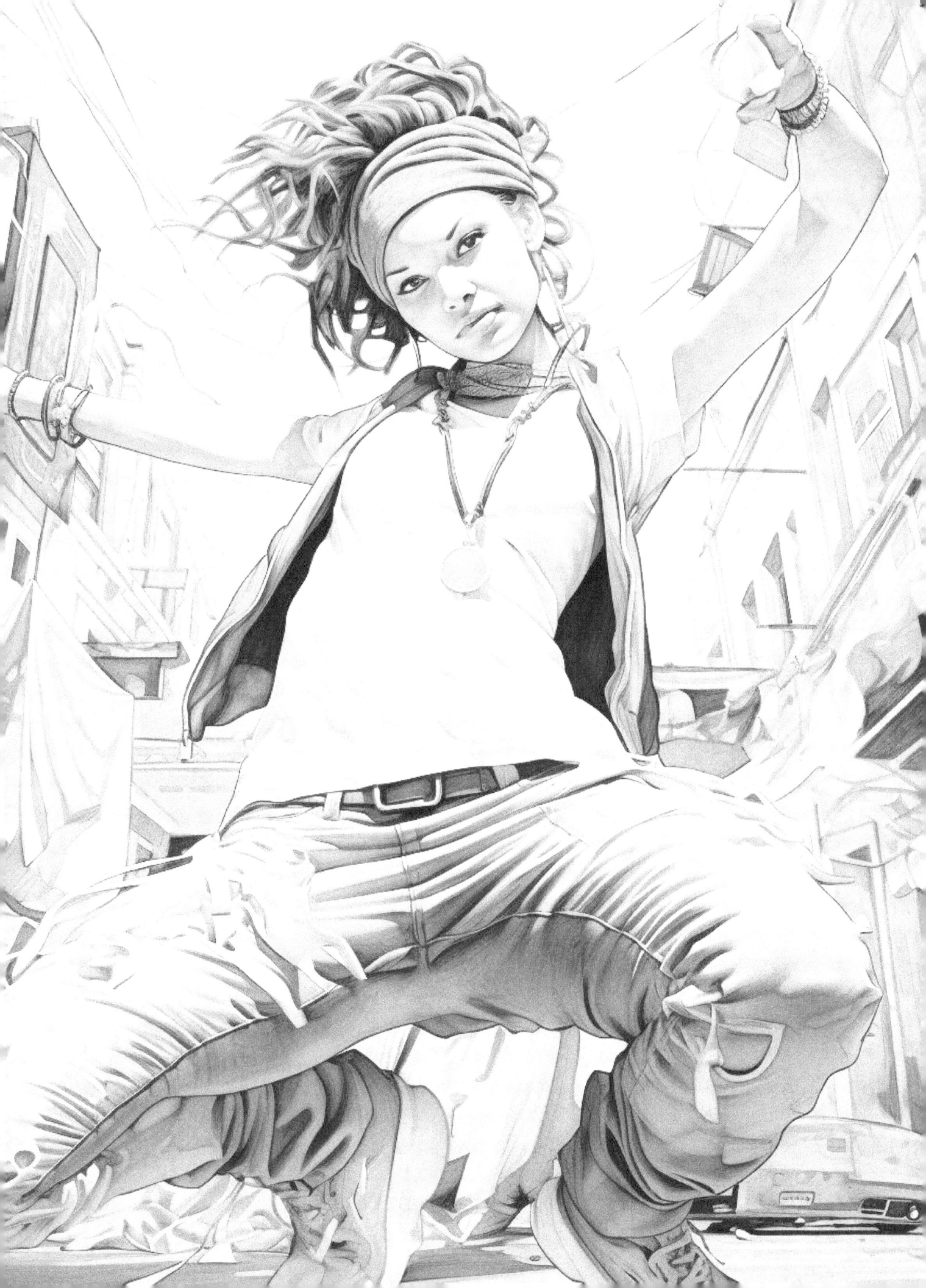

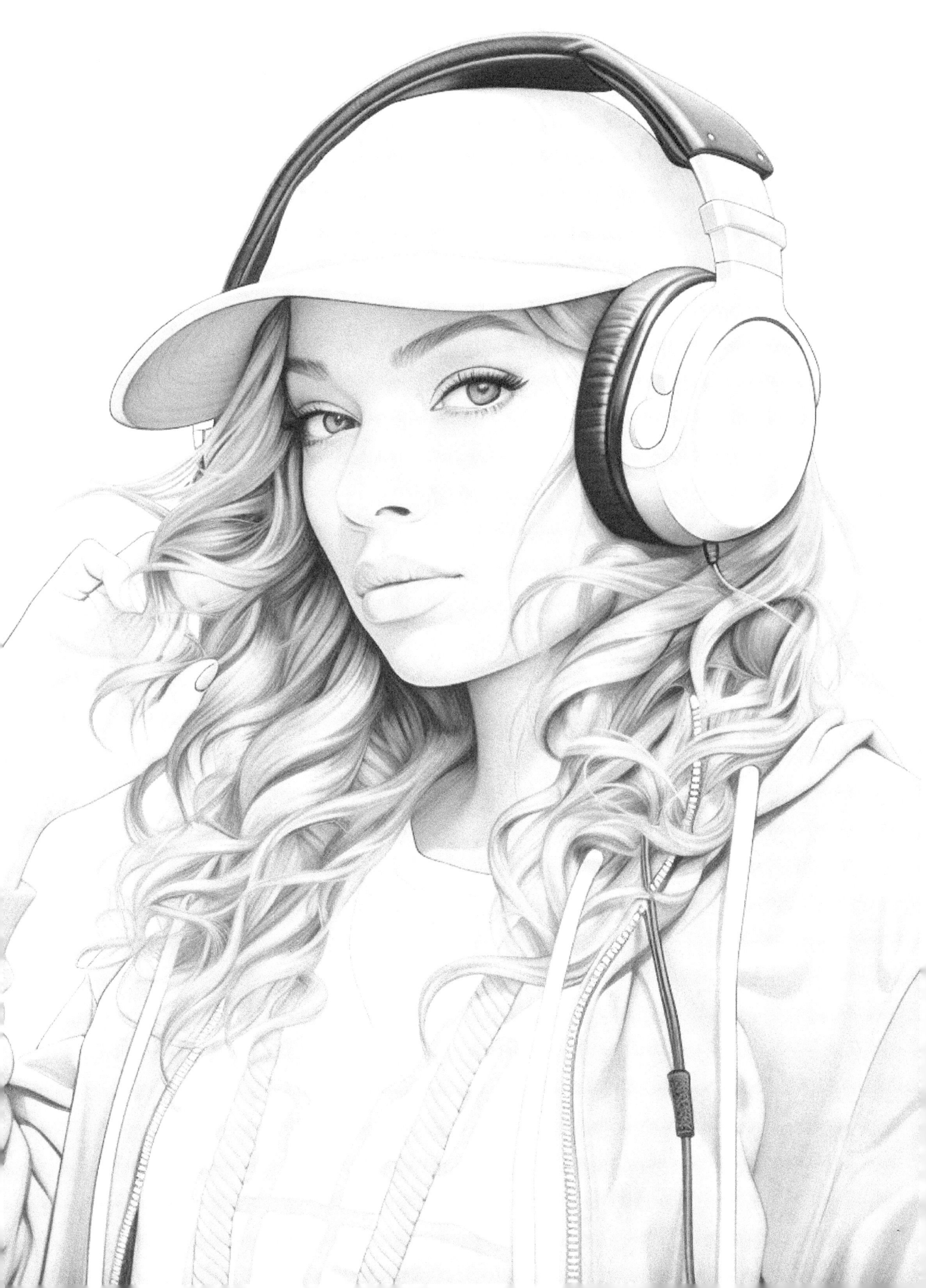

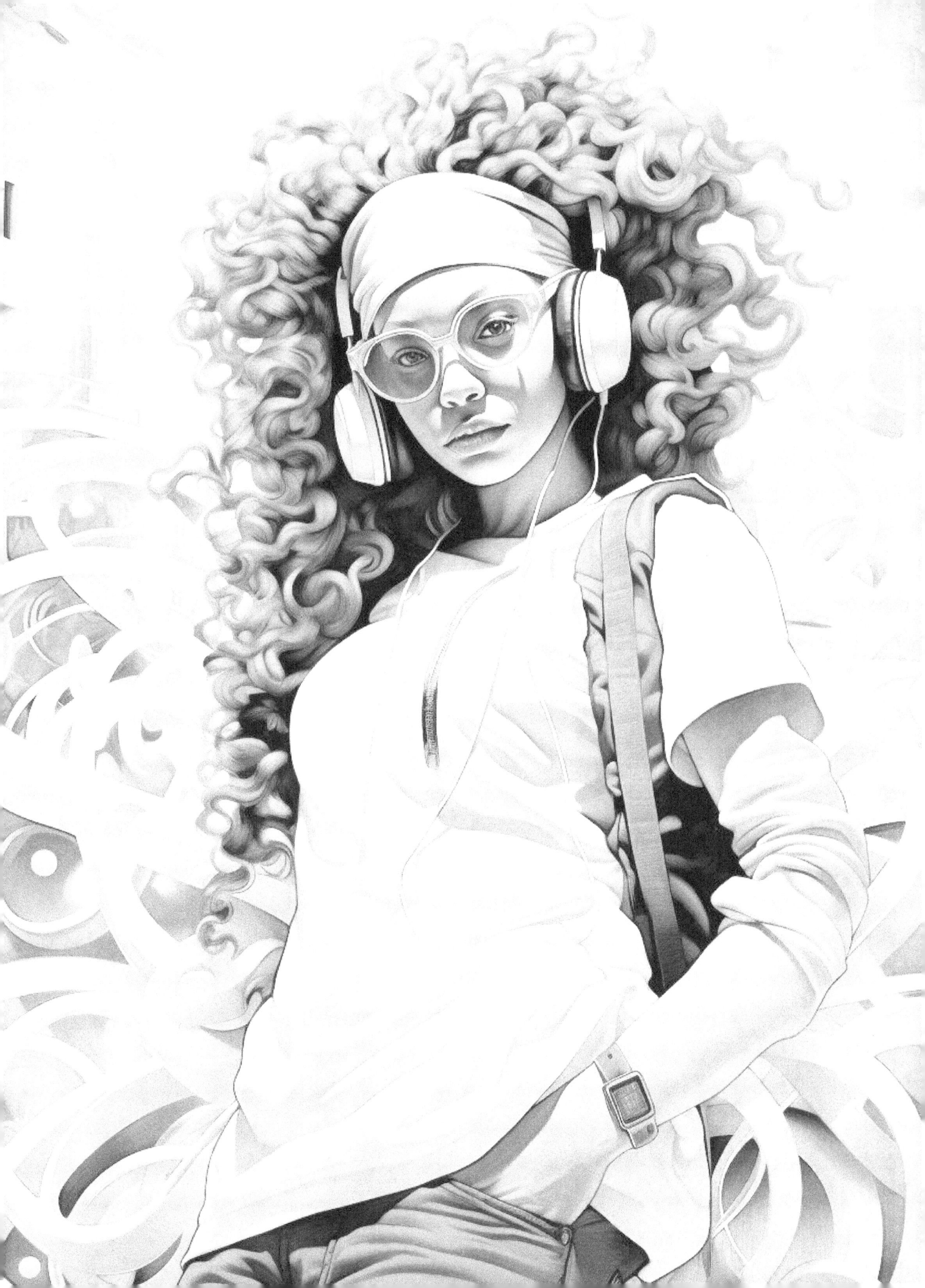

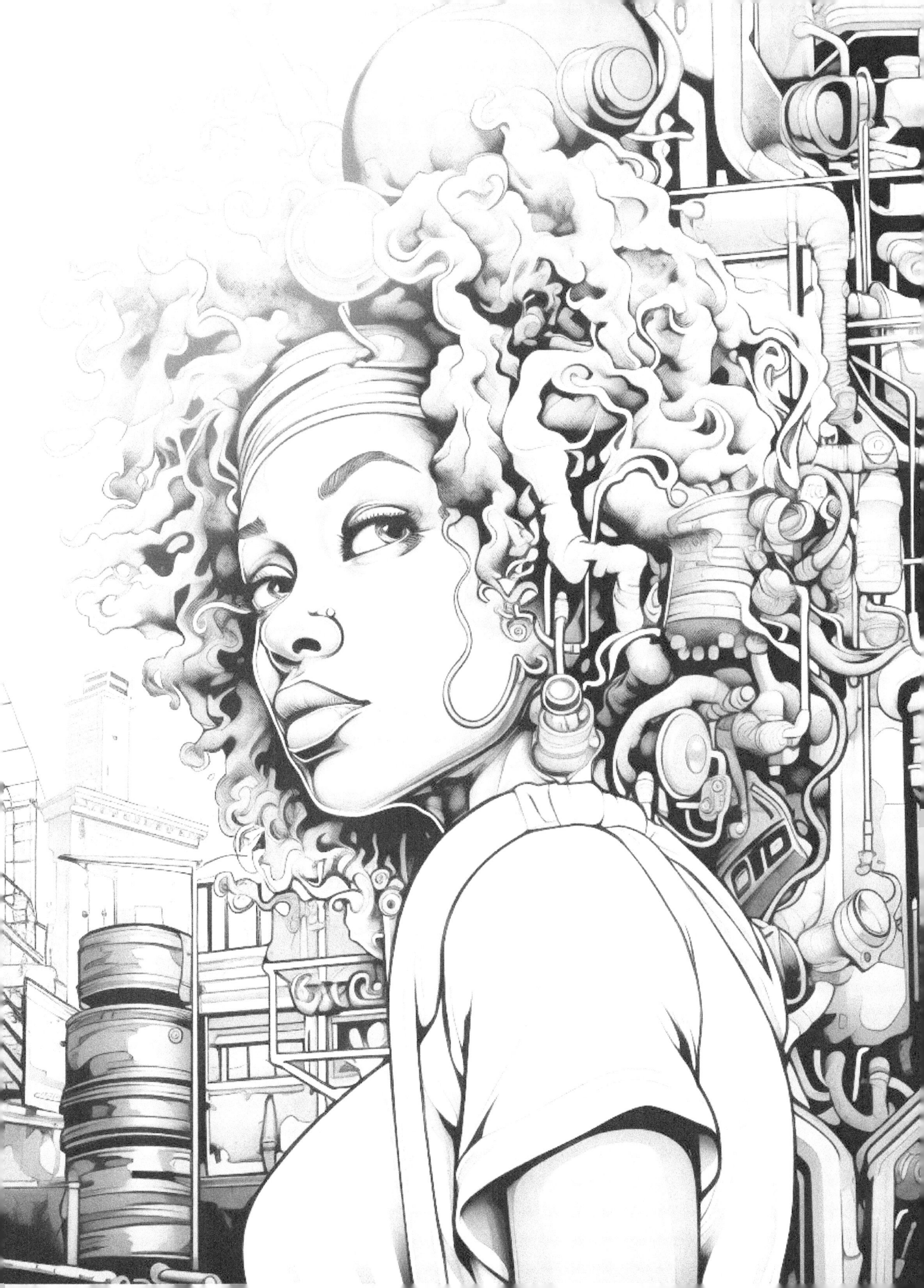

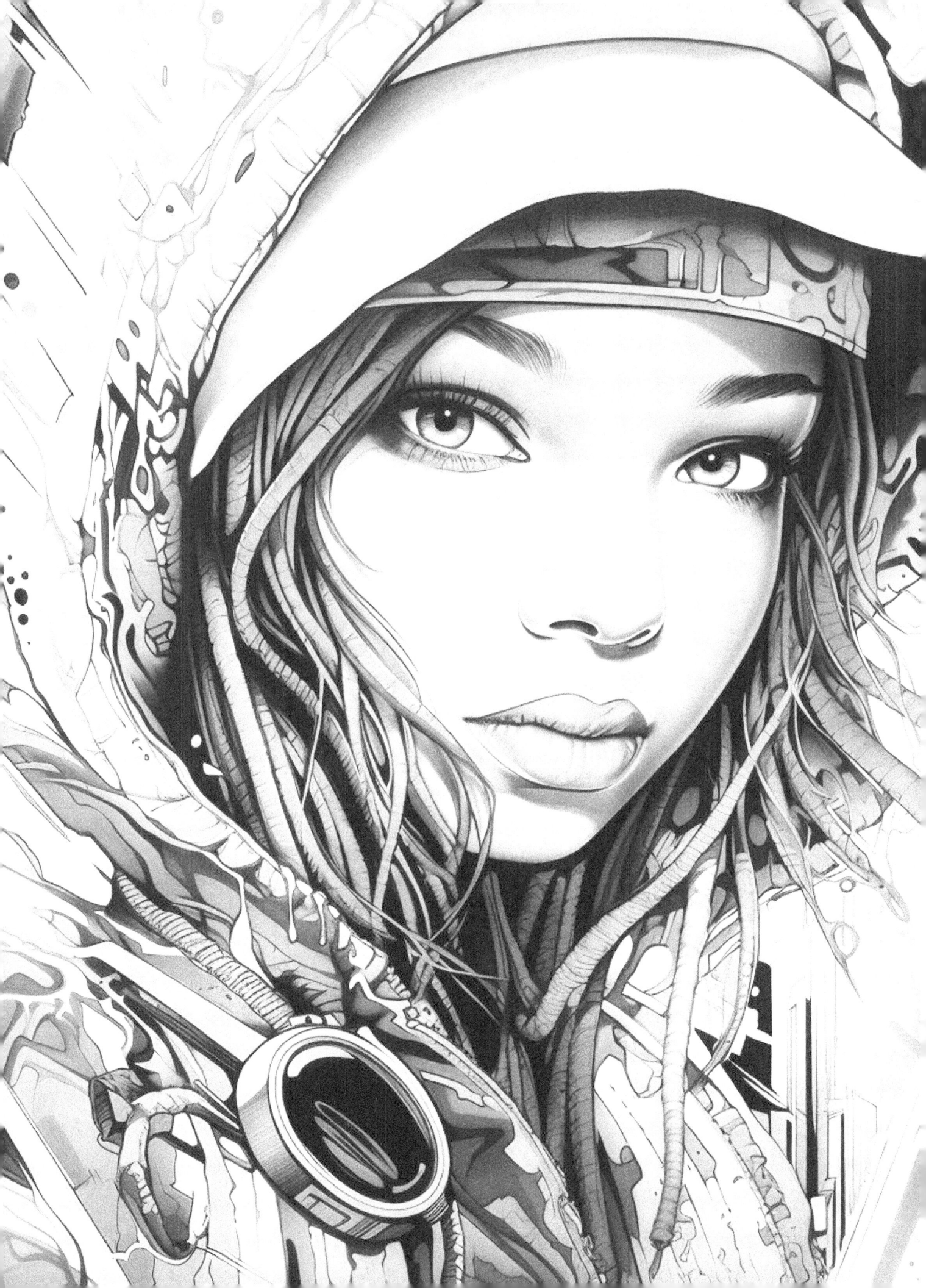

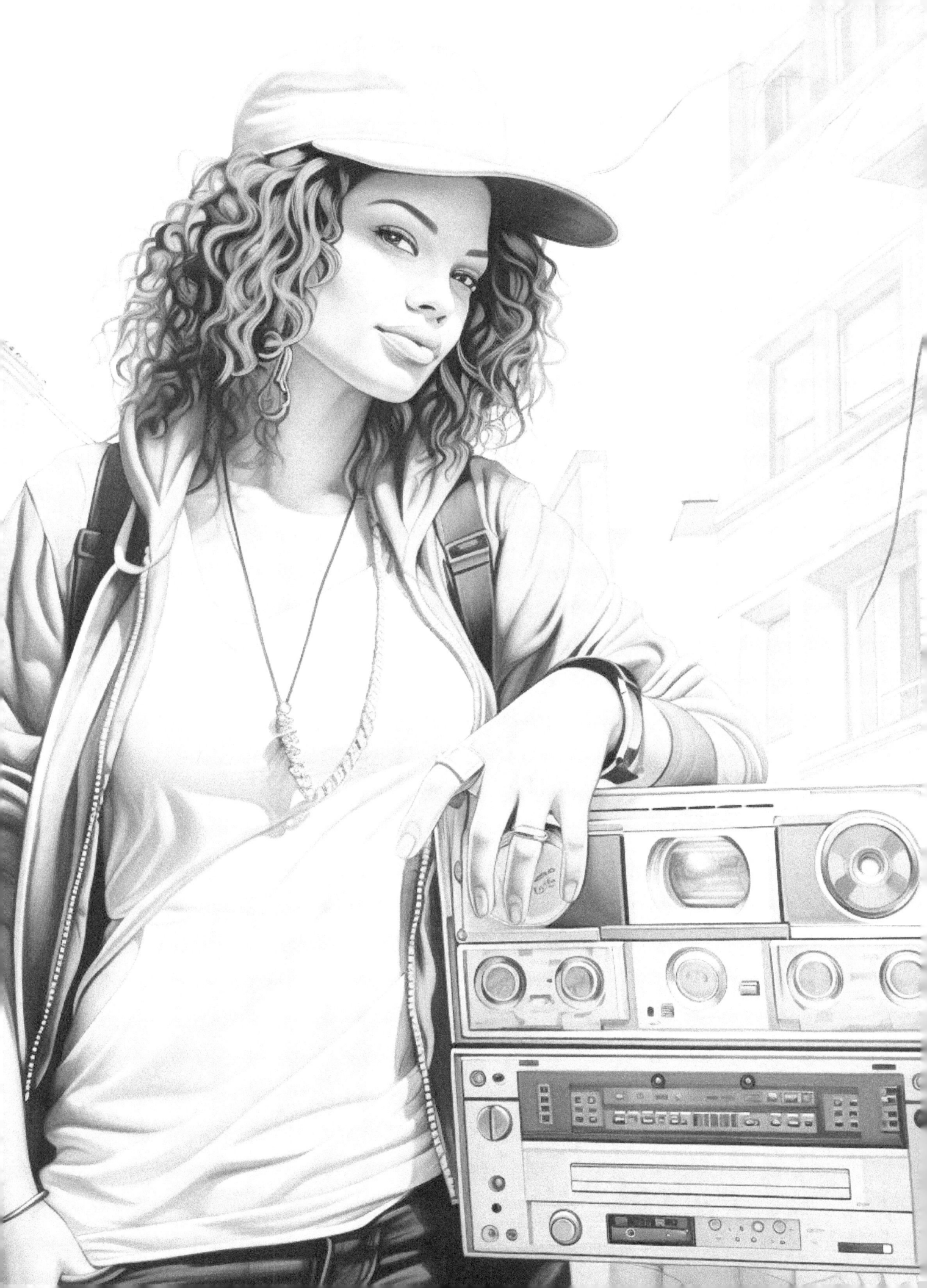

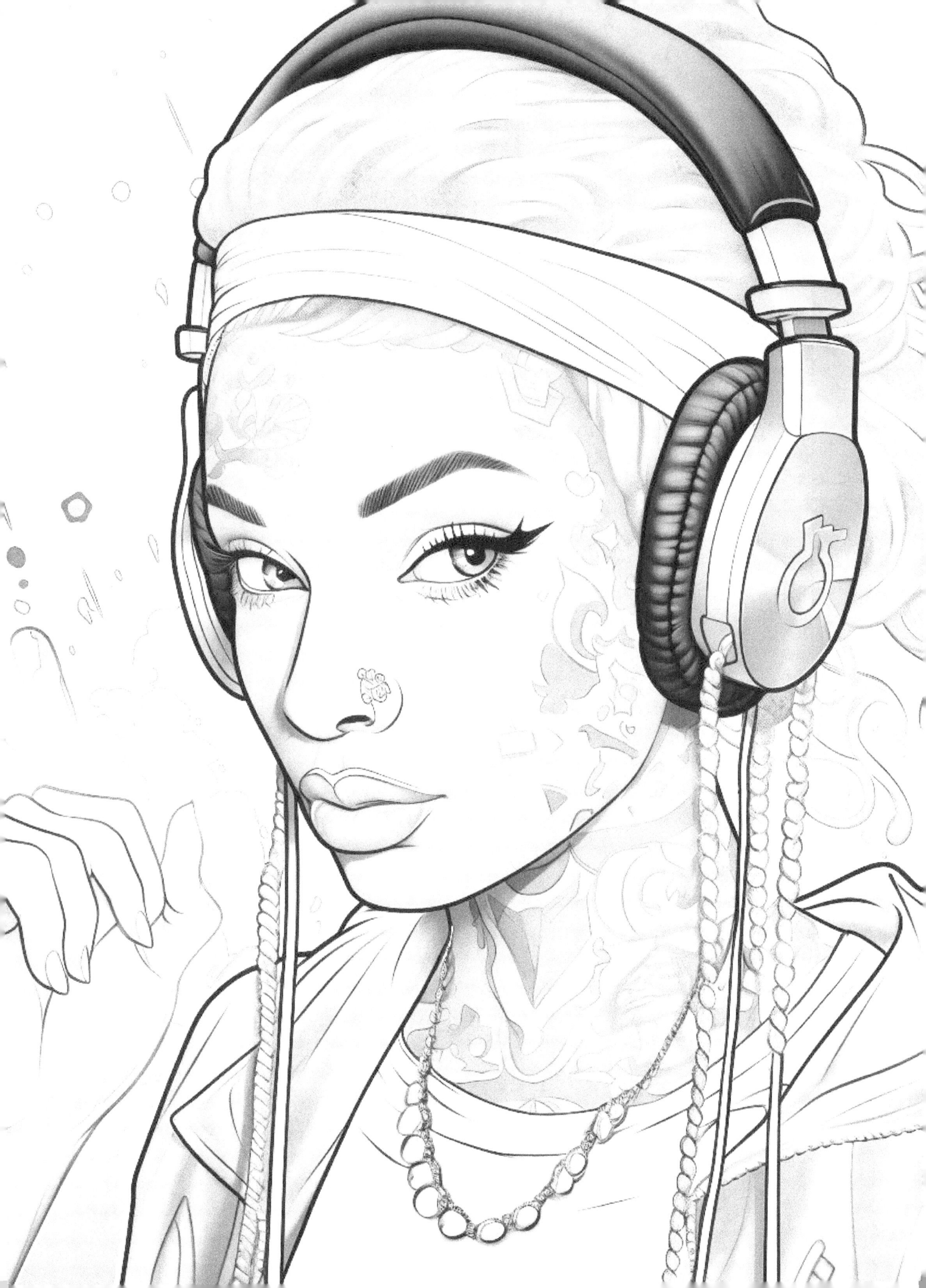

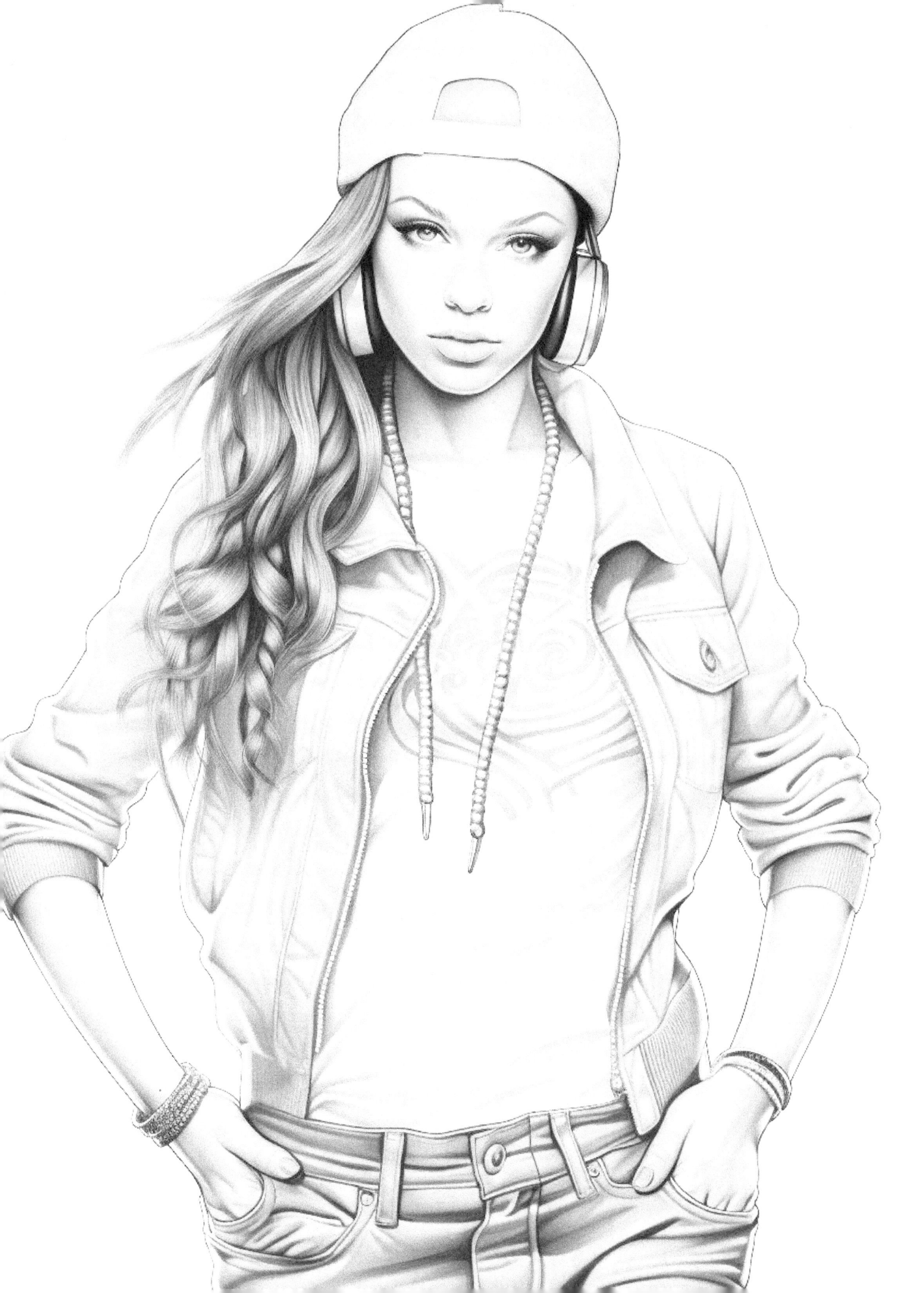

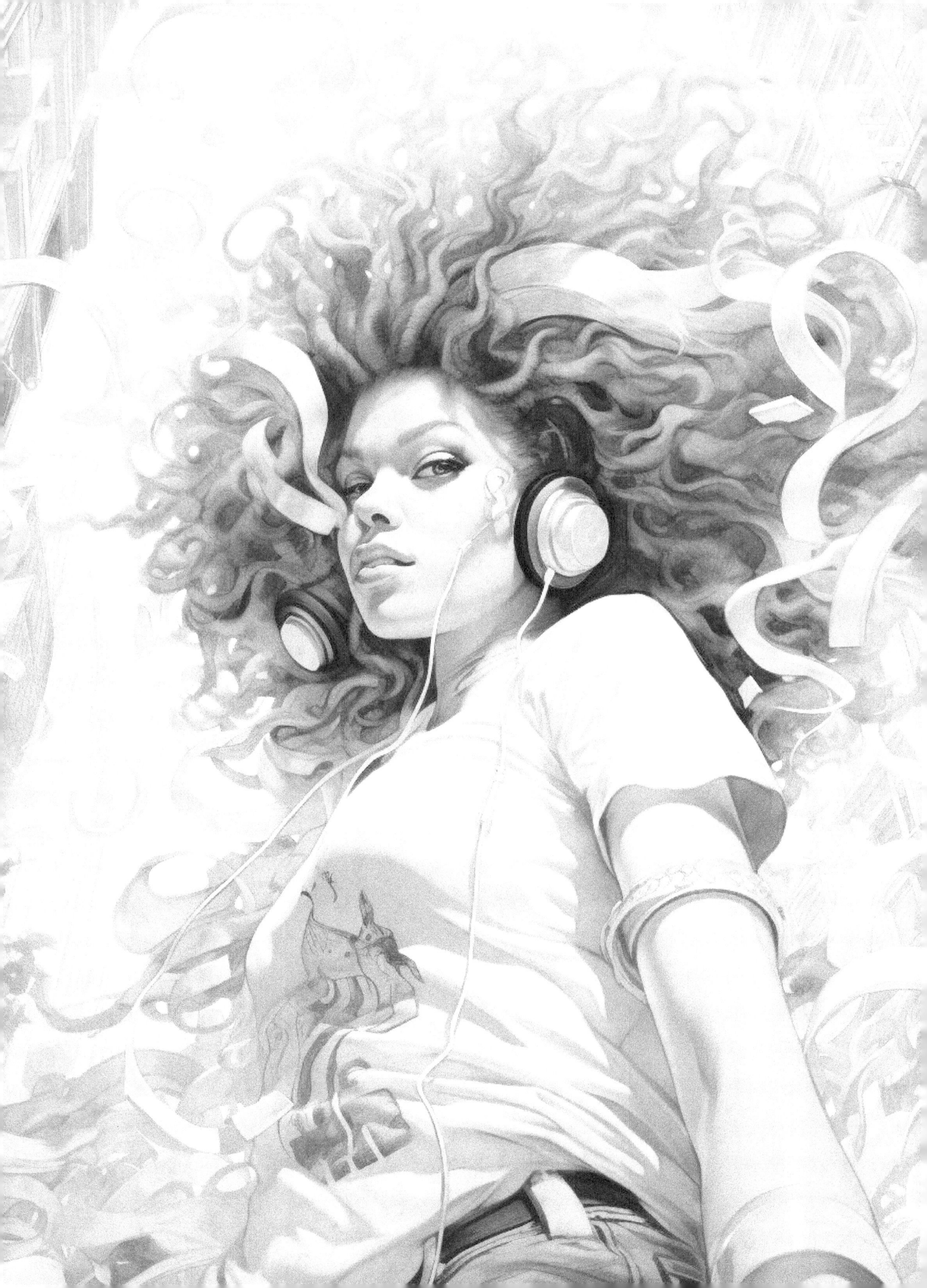

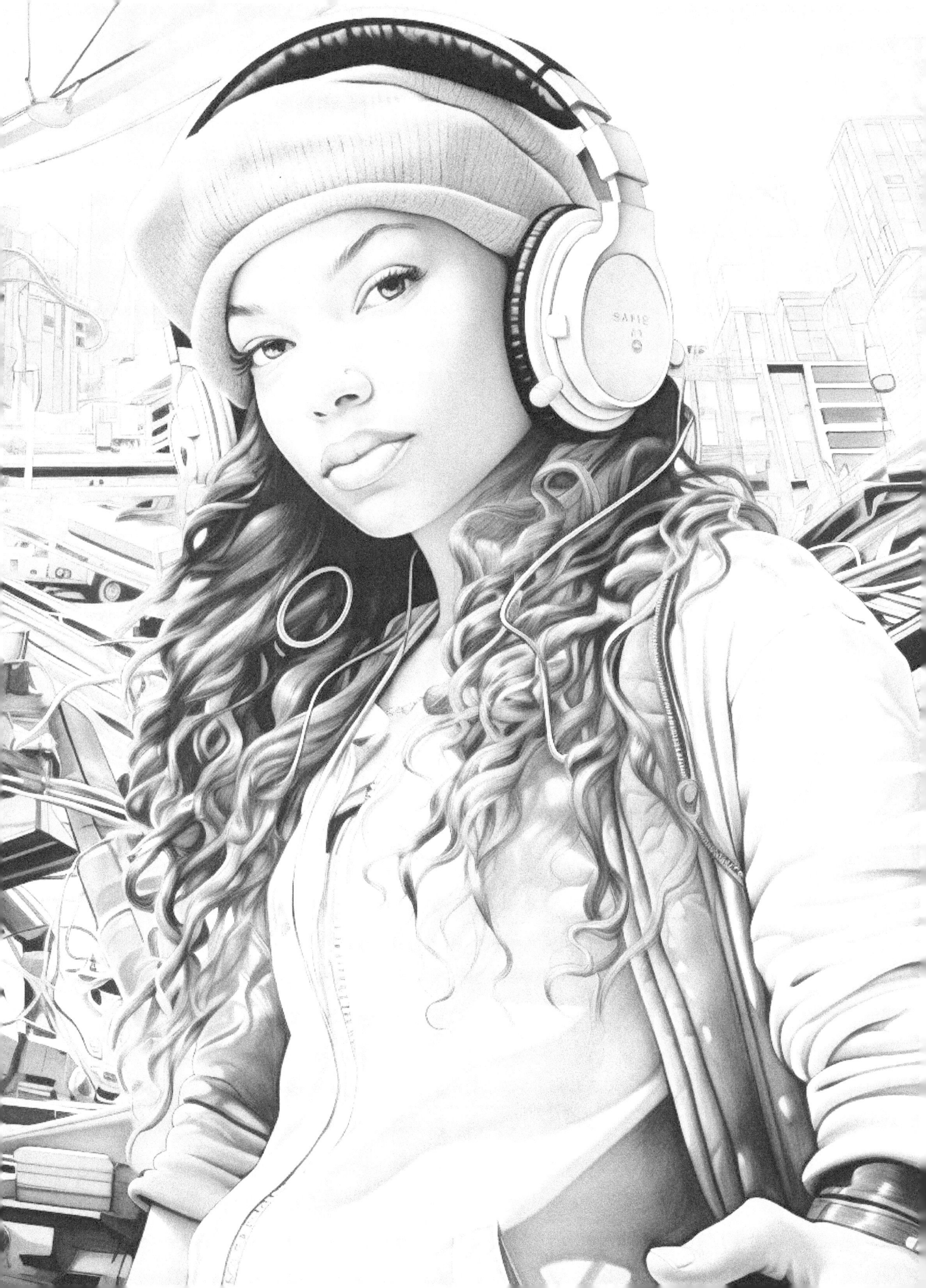

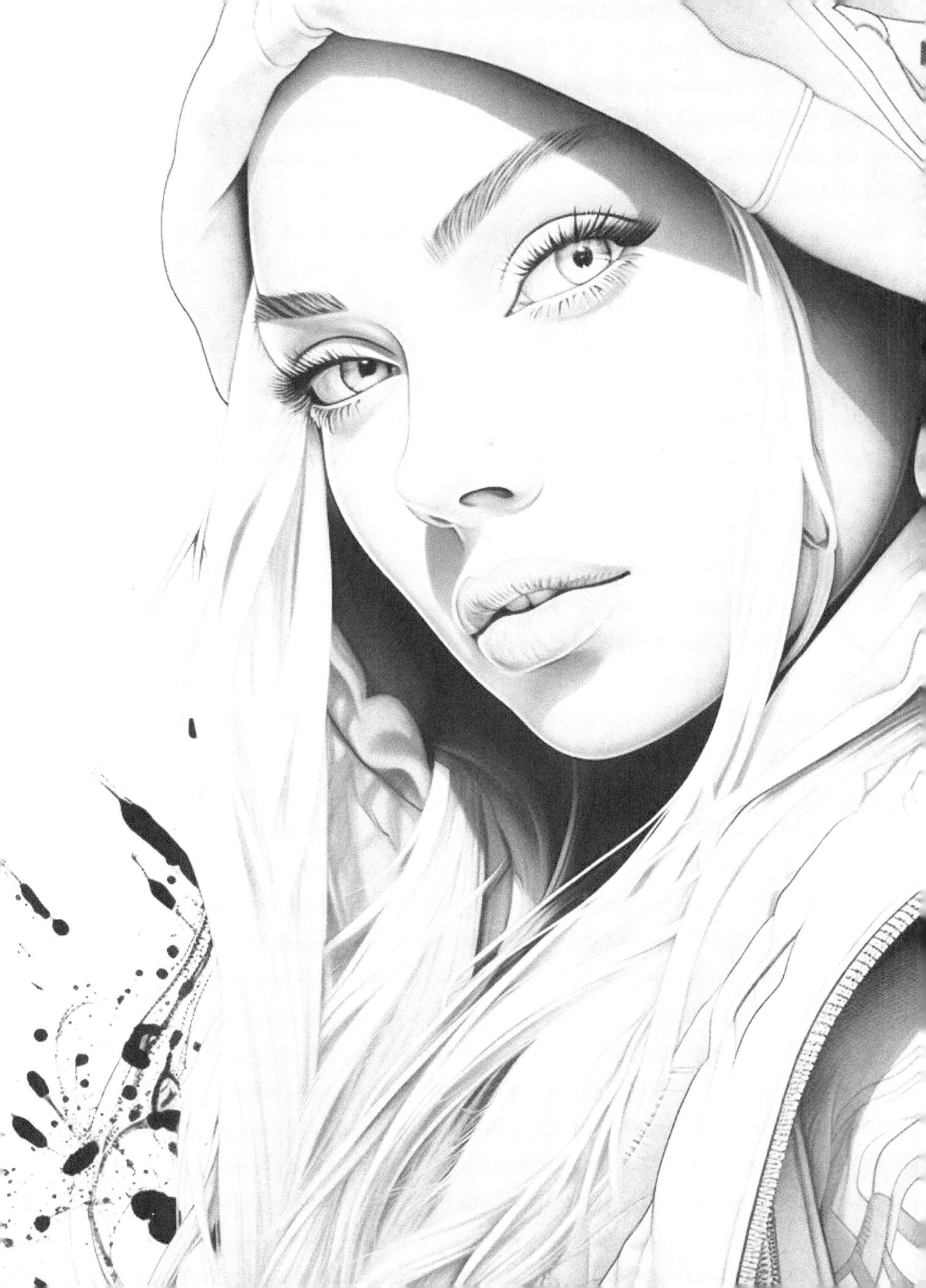

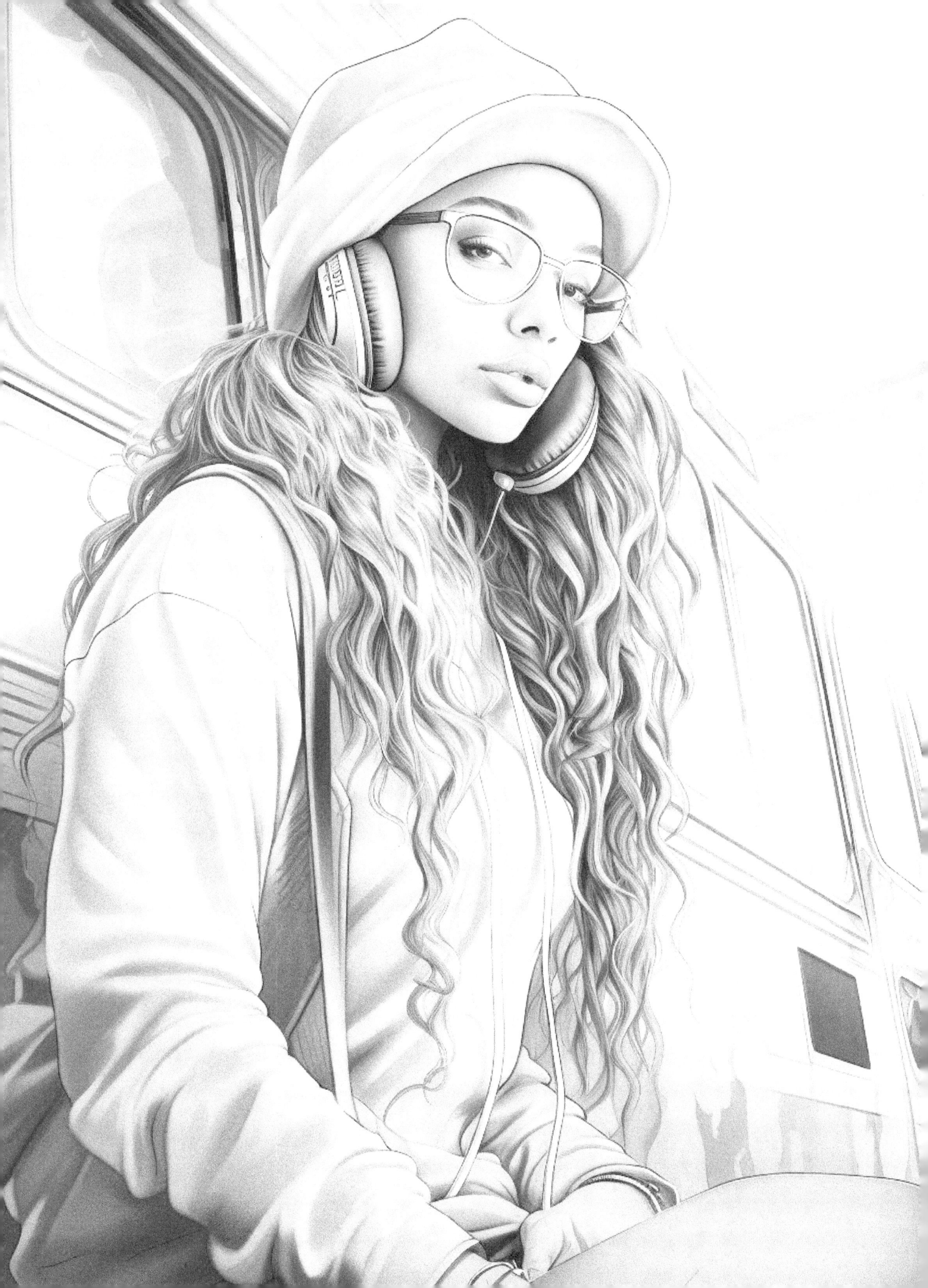

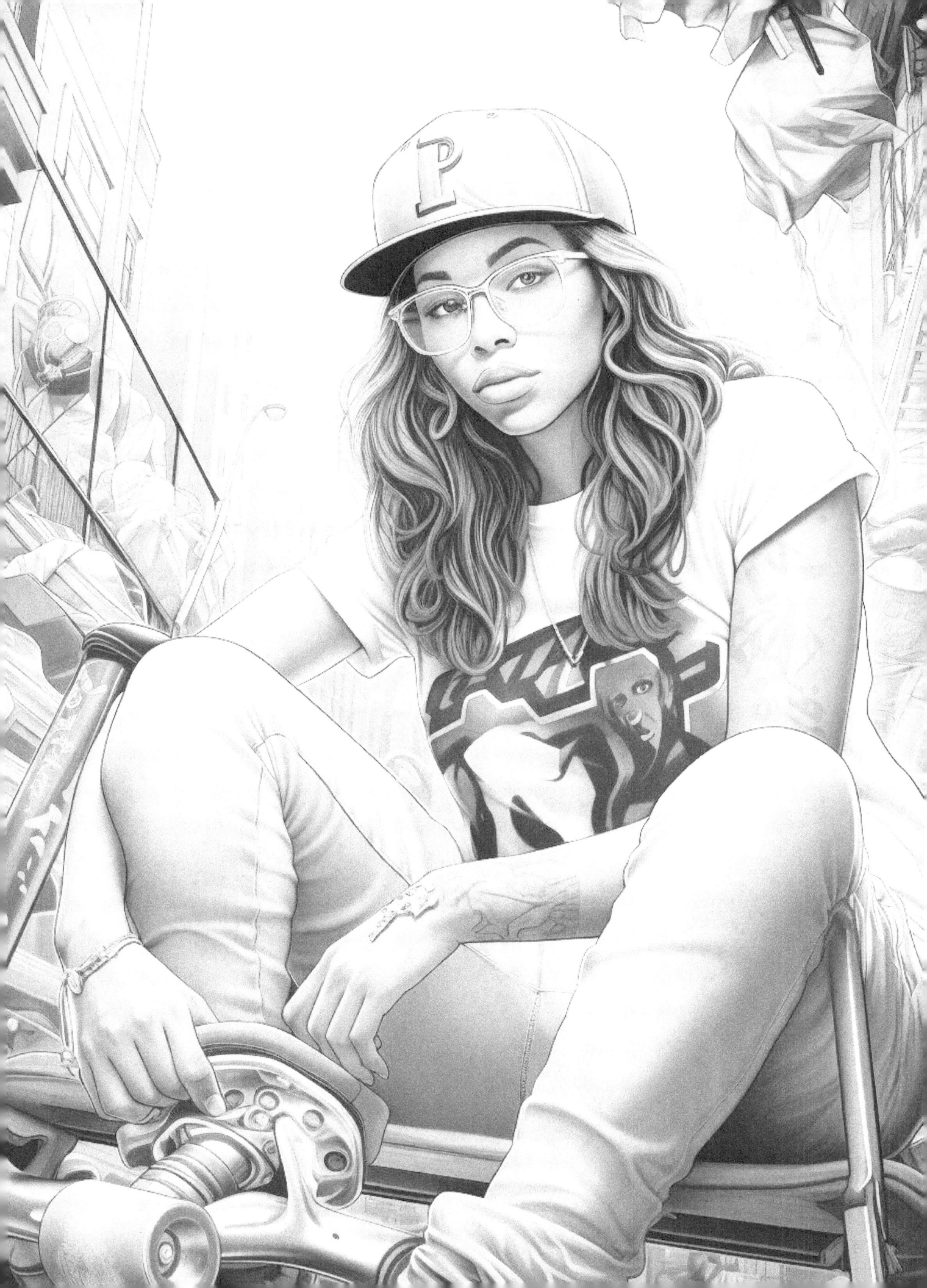

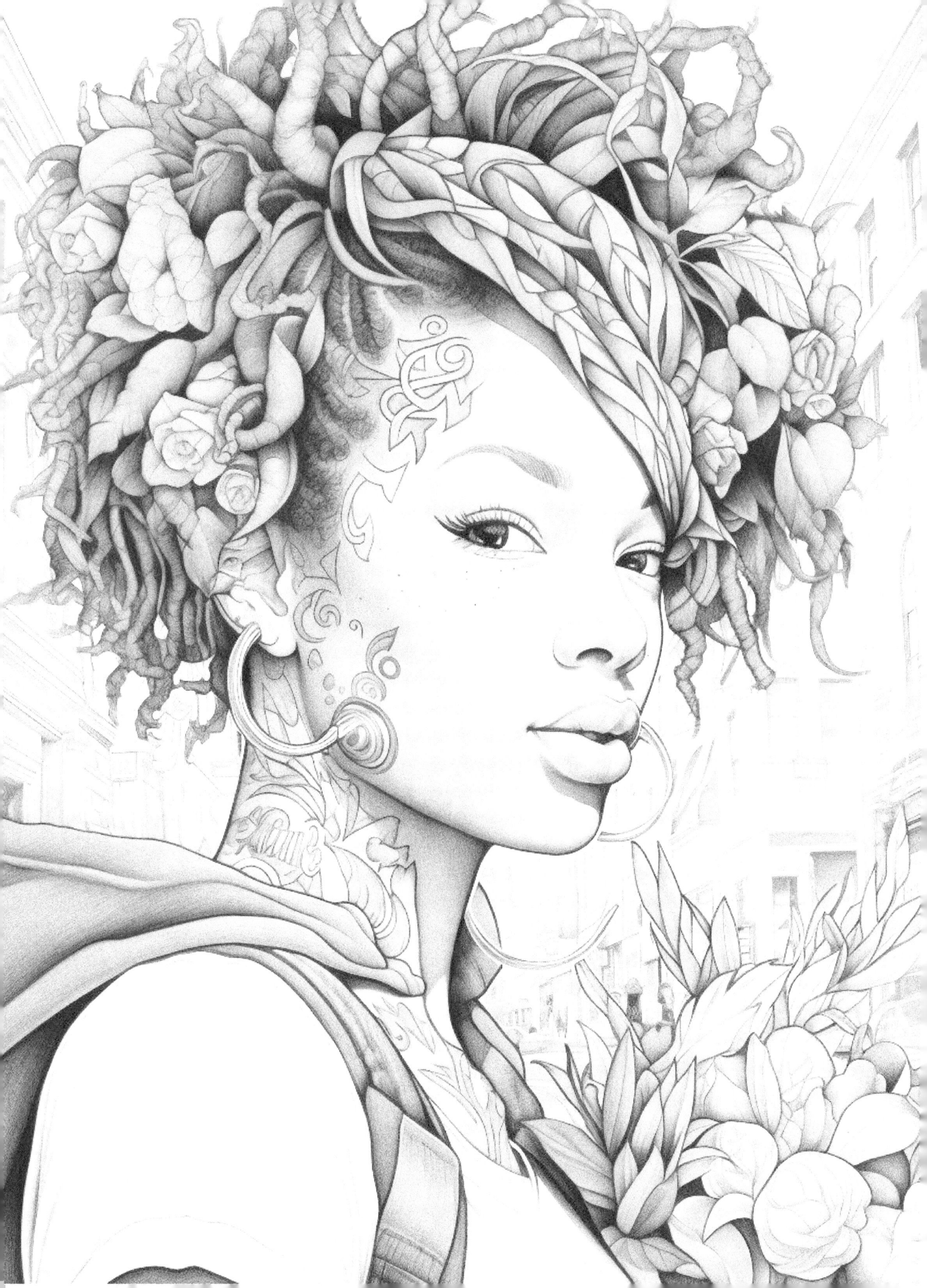

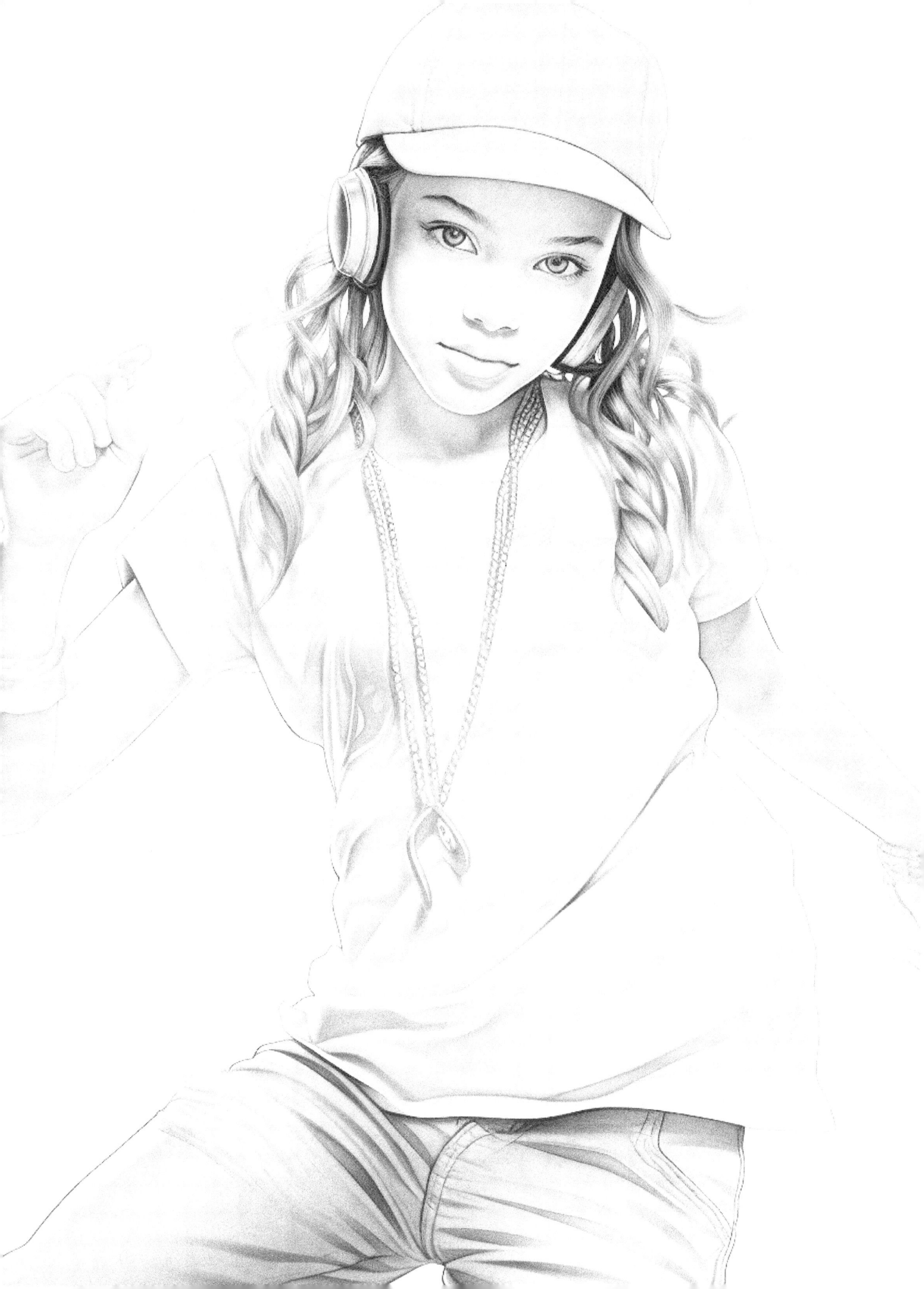

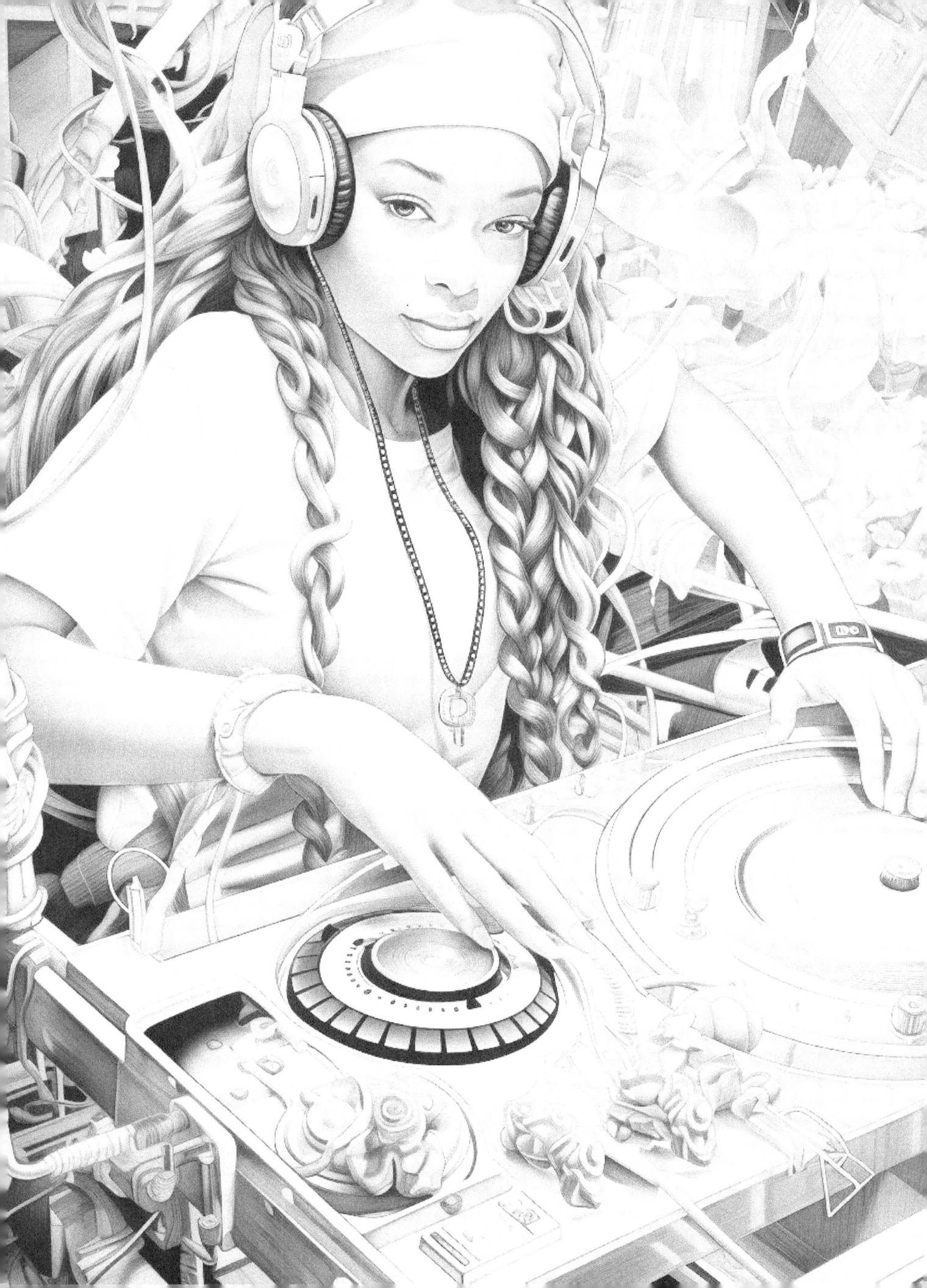

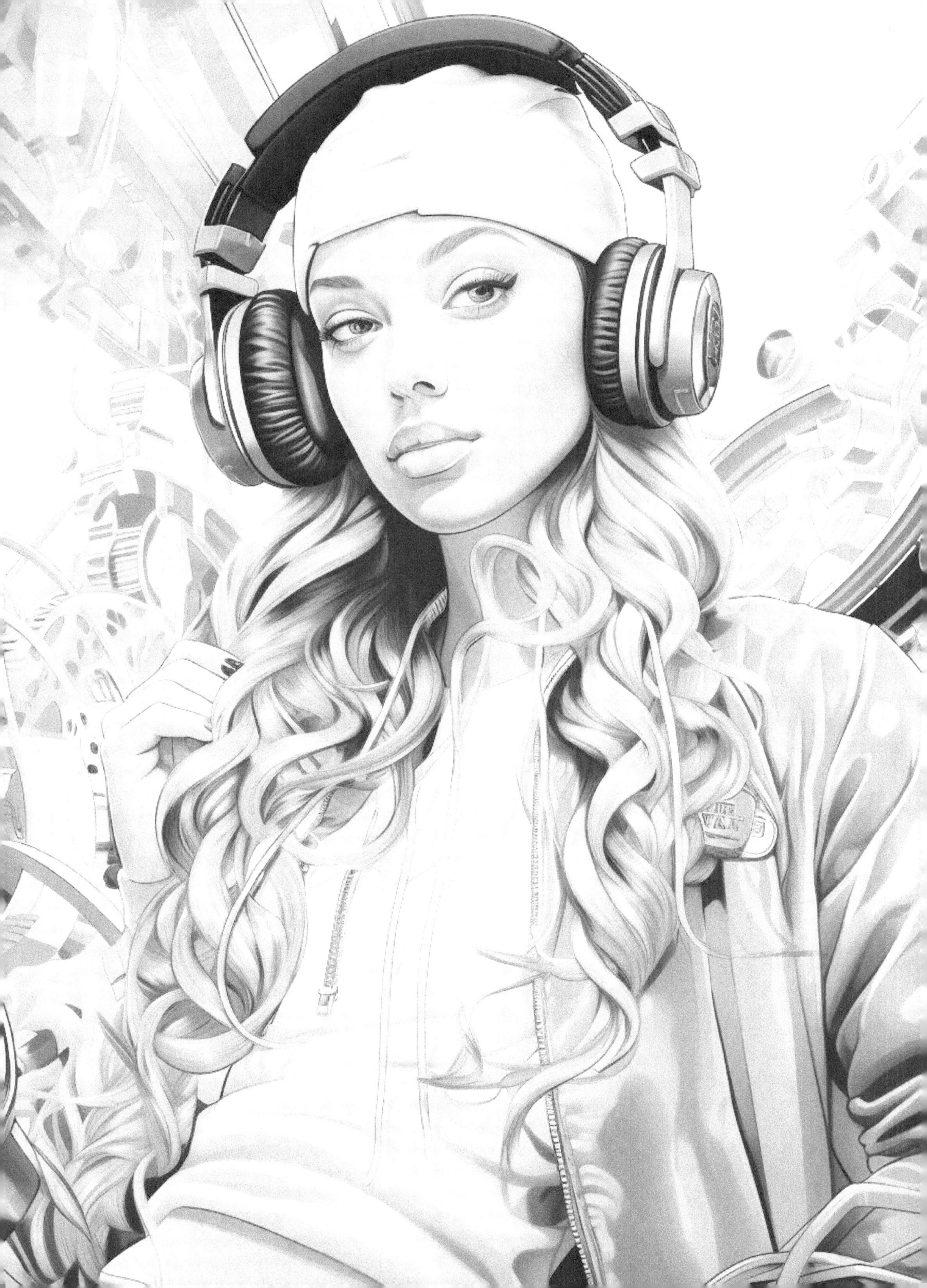

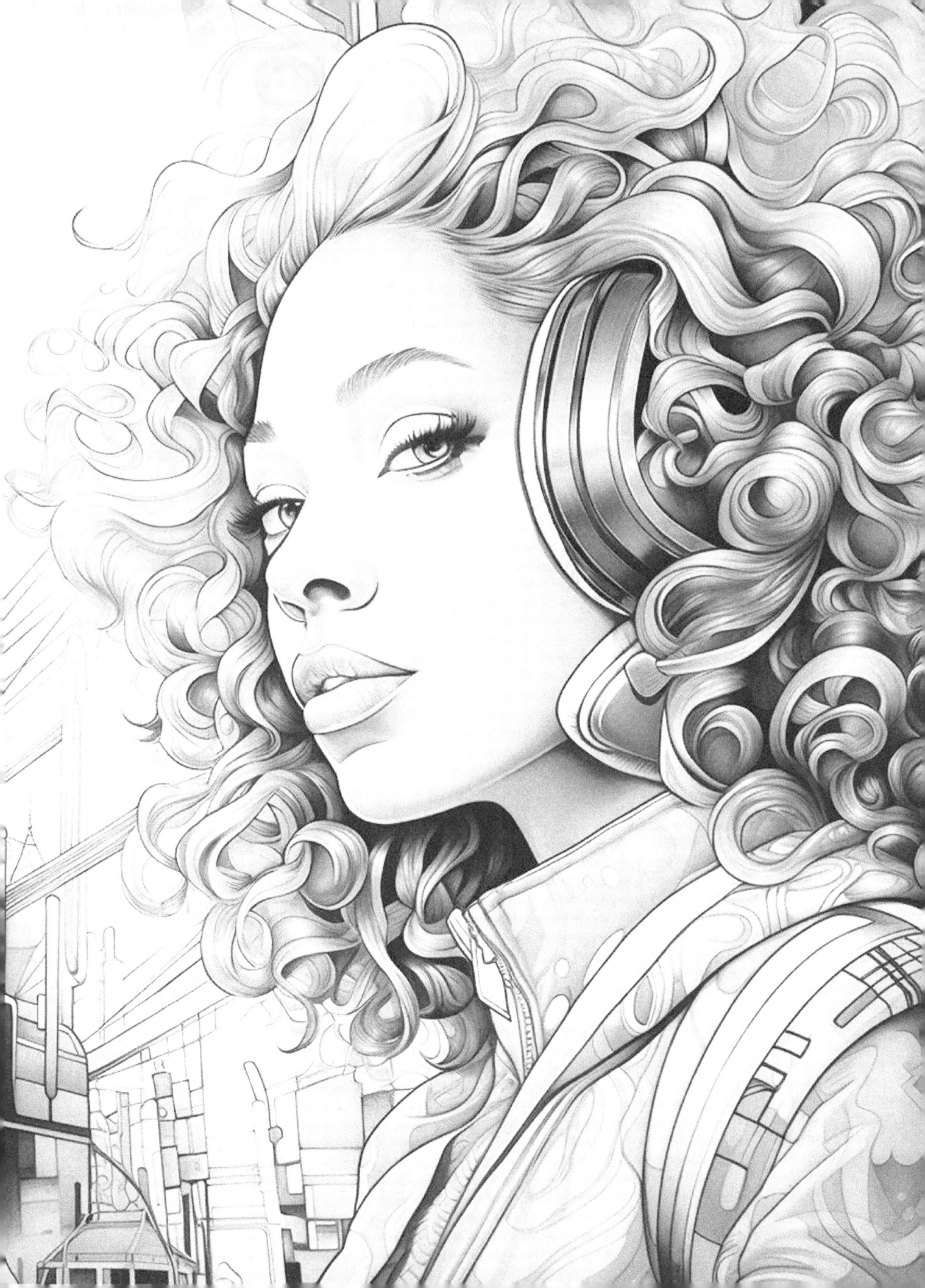

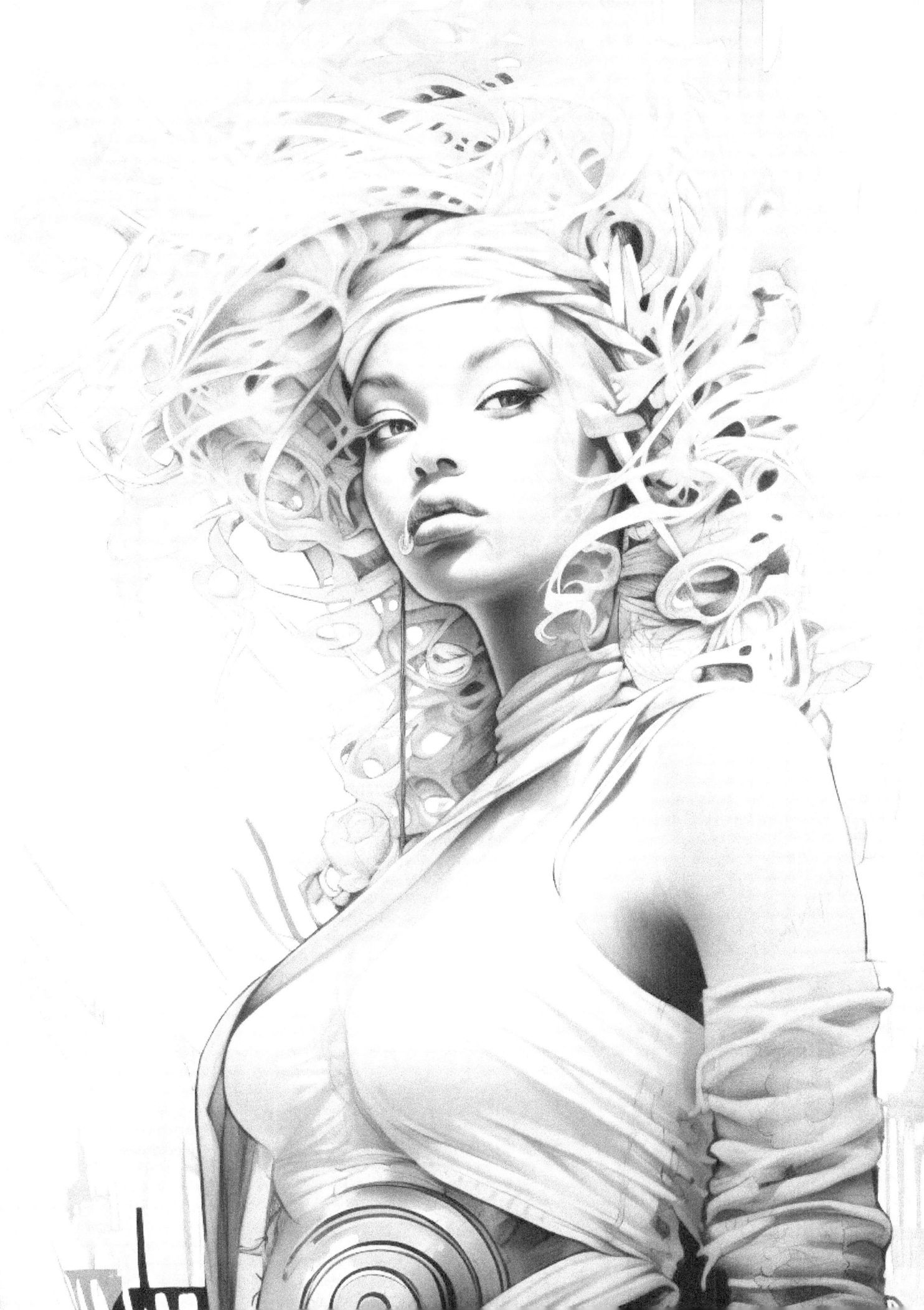

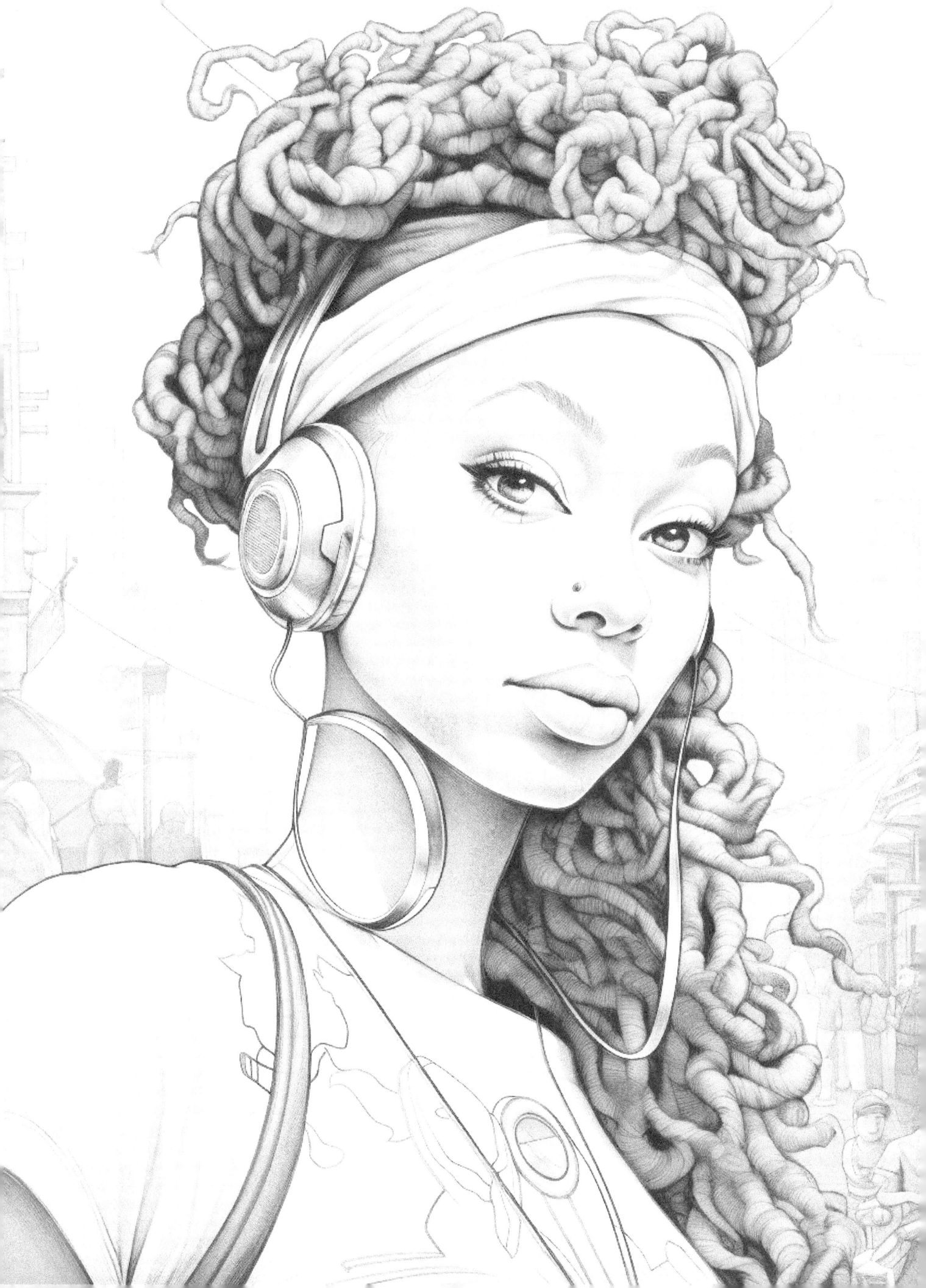

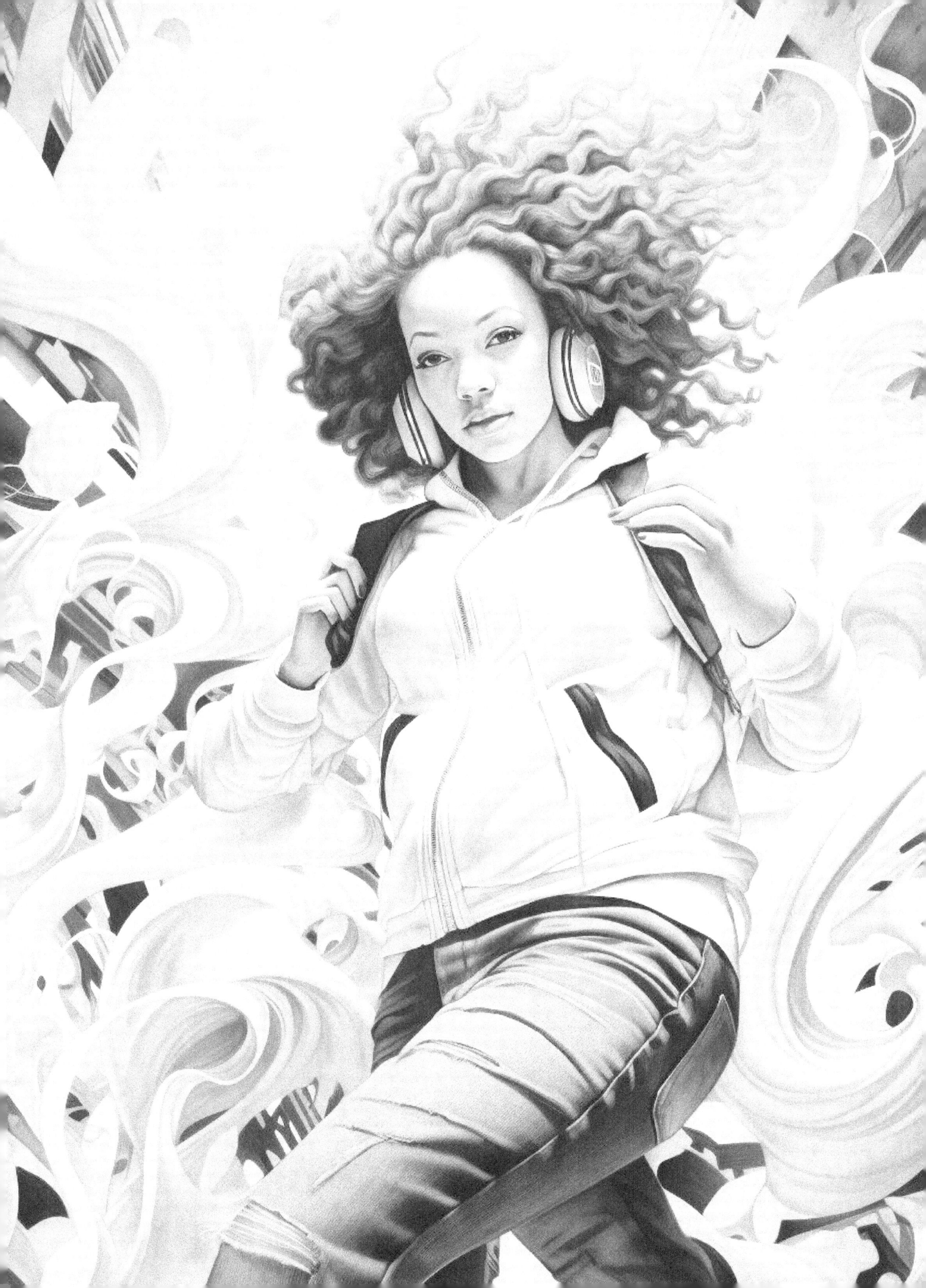

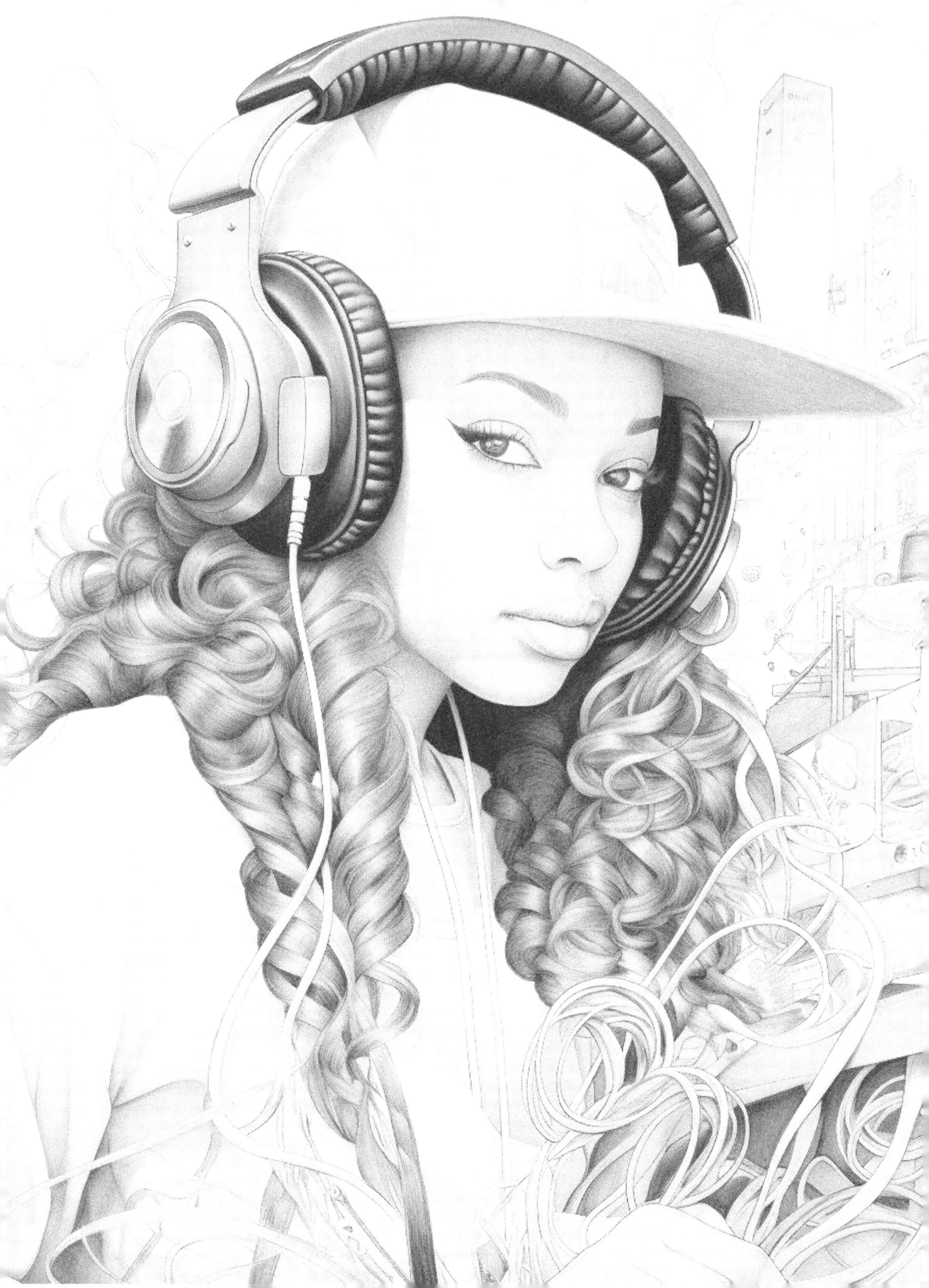

"If you enjoyed our product, it would be greatly appreciated if you could leave a review so others can receive the same benefits you have. Your review will help us see what is and what isn't working so we can serve you better and all our other customers even more."

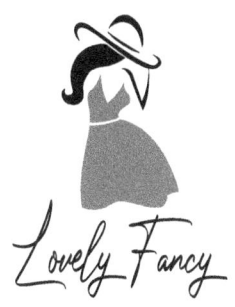

Lovely Fancy

For more beautiful books
Please scan the QR code to access
the Amazon page

Feminine Elegance Across Cultures: A Timeless Portrait Coloring Books

Fantasy Femmes: Pretty Women's Portraits Coloring Journey